Assessment in Business Education

National Business Education Association Yearbook, No. 38

2000

Editor:
Jim Rucker
Fort Hays University
Hays, Kansas

Assistant Editor:
Ramona J. Schoenrock
Columbus High School
Columbus, Nebraska

Published by:
National Business Education Association
1914 Association Drive
Reston, VA 20191-1596
703-860-8300 • Fax: 703-620-4483
www.nbea.org

Assessment in Business Education

National Business Education Association
1914 Association Drive
Reston, VA 20191-1596

ISBN 0-933964-54-4

PREFACE

Do you remember this testing scenario? Students, with #2 pencils in hand, bubbling in circles, racing against time to answer questions designed to test their knowledge of the subject matter.

The traditional paper-and-pencil tests may validate learning, but the concept of testing has a new meaning today. Our complex, global society demands an increasingly sophisticated array of skills in future workers, and new assessment strategies have evolved to measure and promote high-quality instruction. As educators move from testing to assessment, it behooves us to examine, review, and evaluate our current procedures. Some important issues we must consider include

- *What is the purpose of the assessment?*

- *Who will conduct the assessment and when?*

- *Is the appropriate assessment tool being used to measure the learning?*

- *What assessment strategies are most useful for monitoring the progress and achievement of an increasingly diverse student population?*

- *How can portfolios be implemented in assessment, and what basic decisions must be addressed in the portfolio design?*

Business educators must accept the ongoing charge of developing and integrating quality assessment strategies into their curricula. Assessment becomes the critical element that measures student understanding, monitors instruction, and forms curriculum decisions. Teachers, students, parents, and the business community depend upon reliable classroom assessment to drive the teaching/learning process and to provide students with the appropriate skills to function effectively in the workplace.

Increased accountability at the local, state, and national levels has elevated the emphasis on student assessment. New assessment standards have also affected teacher preparation and practice. This places an immense responsibility on administrators, teachers, and learners to improve educational outcomes. Educators are asked to set high standards for their students. Performance standards, such as the National Standards for Business Education, have been formulated to guide instruction and assessment.

Consequently, it is very timely that NBEA publish a yearbook that examines the implications of assessment, assessment design, and multiple assessment tools. Assessment bears an intensifying role of importance today and has become an integral aspect of teaching and learning.

This Yearbook can serve as a catalyst for you to analyze and revise your assessment procedures. It has been written for the novice and experienced teacher, curriculum consultant, and administrator with a methodical approach to ensure quality assessment in business education.

The sections of the Yearbook are designed to assist in developing and implementing a plan of assessment strategies for the business education curriculum. The chapters contribute to the purpose, process, and products of assessment. Several chapters contain various examples of assessment that you may adapt for your particular needs.

We would like to express our appreciation to those who contributed to the 2000 Yearbook. The editors extend special recognition to the chapter authors, the reviewers, the NBEA Publications Committee, and the NBEA publications staff.

Please note that the listed Web site addresses were accurate when the chapters were written but may have changed since publication.

Jim Rucker, Editor
Fort Hays University
Hays, Kansas

and

Ramona J. Schoenrock, Assistant Editor
Columbus High School
Columbus, Nebraska

TABLE OF CONTENTS

Part III: Assessment—The Key to Effective Learning

Part IV: Partners in Assessment

Part V: Assessment in the Business Education Curriculum

James Russell Smith, Jr.
North Carolina Department of Public Instruction
Raleigh, North Carolina

ACKNOWLEDGMENTS

The following business educators devoted their time, effort, and expertise to reviewing the 2000 NBEA Yearbook, *Assessment in Business Education*:

R. Jon Ackley
Virginia Commonwealth University
Richmond, Virginia

Betty S. Johnson
Stephen F. Austin State University
Nacogdoches, Texas

Sharon Andelora
Woodcliff School
Woodcliff Lake, New Jersey

Arthur McEntee
University of Maine at Machias
Machias, Maine

Lloyd Bartholome
Utah State University
Logan, Utah

Gearldine Modrell
Program Supervisor
Office of Superintendent of
Public Instruction
Olympia, Washington

Lisa Bourlier
University of Nebraska-Lincoln
Independent Study High School
Lincoln, Nebraska

Linda Morgan
Eastern Oklahoma State College
Wilburton, Oklahoma

Joyce Caton
Fontbonne College
St. Louis, Missouri

Kay Orrell
Allan Hancock College
Santa Maria, California

Judith Durish
Daytona Beach Community College
Daytona Beach, Florida
and
St. Johns River Community College
St. Augustine, Florida

Marilyn Price
Kirkwood Community College
Cedar Rapids, Iowa

Bonnie Sibert
Nebraska State Department of Education
Lincoln, Nebraska

Lonnie Echternacht
University of Missouri-Columbia
Columbia, Missouri

Wanda L. Stitt-Gohdes
University of Georgia
Athens, Georgia

Shirley Eiken
Winona State University
Winona, Minnesota

Janet Scaglione
University of South Florida
Tampa, Florida

Kenneth L. Gorman
Winona State University
Winona, Minnesota

John Swope
East Carolina University
Greenville, North Carolina

Wally Guyot
Fort Hays State University
Hays, Kansas

Bonnie Roe White
Auburn University
Auburn, Alabama

Janice Hopper
Century High School
Santa Ana, California

Assessment in Education—The Past, Present, and Future

Susan R. Hatfield and Kenneth L. Gorman
Winona State University
Winona, Minnesota

No question in academic circles has elicited more interest, concern, frustration, and anxiety than "How are our students doing?" The interest is widespread as legislators, accrediting bodies, and the general public are all demanding that educational institutions justify themselves in terms of outcomes related to the investments made by federal and state governments, parents, and students. Administrators and faculty, overwhelmed by the wide array of assessment tools and methodologies, are concerned about how this emphasis on assessment will translate into meeting graduation and accreditation standards and how it will impact budgeting.

Marchese's (1993) comments related to assessment in higher education are equally applicable to secondary education:

> ... Education institutions must monitor the quality of the goods and services they provide to be able to improve continuously—which means that people in those organizations must systematically keep track of how the organization is doing and that the resulting information must be readily available to all within the organization. Decisions in (higher) education often have been made or influenced by personal impression, anecdote, or complaint. Instead, the quality principle "decisions based on fact" urges (higher) education to "keep track, dig out the facts, find the systemic problem or root cause." (p. 12)

In the past, educational institutions, especially private schools, two-year postsecondary institutions, and colleges/universities would survive only if they managed their enrollments effectively. More recently, public secondary schools have also become enrollment conscious because of voucher plans and postsecondary enrollment options available to high school students.

No one ever used to question whether or how students were changed as the result of the educational experience. Everyone took for granted that some learning took place, but no one measured what kind of learning, how much learning, or even how the learning happened. The days of not being accountable for the learning experience and the subsequent outcomes are gone.

While there are significant advantages to institutions that manage enrollments effectively, ongoing documentation of student learning is now the essential survival skill for educational institutions. Not only do institutions need to continue to enroll and eventually graduate students, but they also need to prove to legislators, accrediting bodies, parents, and the students themselves that education at the different levels has provided the essential skills, knowledge, and values of an educated person.

The History of Assessment

Assessment, as it is currently known, started in the field of psychology during the late 1930s as a result of the work of Henry A. Murry (Peterson, 1999). Focused on determining the skills and knowledge of individuals, Murry and his colleagues developed a series of tests and other means of evaluating performance and making decisions about intervention (Hartle, 1986). The study of assessment led to the idea that assessing a client's existing condition is necessary in order to provide appropriate treatment.

Multimethod multitrait assessment has been traced to the military during World War II by Hartle (1986). During the war, selected soldiers participated in a series of tests, examinations, activities, and interviews to determine which soldiers had the best chance of becoming officers.

Following World War II, assessment became part of business and industry as organizations, following the lead of the earlier military model of multimethod assessment, established assessment procedures to measure the skills, abilities, aptitudes, and attitudes of current and potential employees. During the 1950s and 1960s, assessment became important to education because of the perception that "a substantial national investment in education was regarded as an insurance policy in the Cold War and as a way to enhance our technological and scientific position in world trade" (Astin, 1993).

In the 1980s, financial, political, and social pressures forced academic institutions to become more accountable for student learning. Assessment was viewed as the answer to meet the demands for both documenting accountability and improving the quality of our nation's educational system.

Astin (1993, p. 2) explains that the pressures facing higher education in particular were the result of the questions posed by the public and legislators

> ... asking whether the soaring costs of higher education are draining off resources that could be better used for other public purposes. Economic pressures have forced legislators to look for programs in which public spending can be cut, and the high level of federal and state investments in higher education underscores the need for better information on how colleges affect students.

Responding to these and other questions, individual states began requiring schools to assess student learning. The issues surrounding accountability were manifested in greater focus on learner outcomes, graduation standards, and a general concern for excellence in education at all levels.

Stiggins (1994) indicates that for secondary schools, assessment has moved from an era of assessment for sorting to an era of assessment for competence:

> In the passing era, assessment was defined as the quantification of student achievement, so scores could be used to sort and rank students from the highest to the lowest achiever. Schools were deemed effective if they produced a dependable rank order of students at the end of the school experience. In the emerging era, assessment is defined in broader terms than just scores and schools are deemed effective only when and if they produce students who can demonstrate certain specified competencies. (p. 20)

Over the past century, standardized testing programs were the primary types of assessment used in secondary schools in the United States. During each of the decades of the 20th century, various types of standardized, centralized testing emerged. In the 1930s scholarship tests were introduced, which ranked students for the purpose of awarding scholarships. National college admission testing programs appeared in the 1940s. Published objective test batteries, which were used at all grade levels, became popular in the 1950s. During the 1970s, statewide testing became widespread; states designed their own tests rather than using published standardized tests. Also, in the 1970s and 1980s, national testing programs became popular (Stiggins, 1994).

Throughout the last third of the 20th century, a different focus—a focus on outcomes—began to emerge. Mastery learning, criterion-reference testing, behavioral outcomes, and competency-based testing became widely used. The era of articulated goals and outcomes, minimum standard attainment, performance-based education, and the assessment of competence emerged to answer the call for accountability (Stiggins, 1994).

In the early 1990s, responding to increasing demands for accountability by the public and legislators, the six regional accrediting bodies for higher education began to require assessment plans for all colleges and universities. Professional accreditation bodies soon followed suit.

Higher education institutions scrambled to respond, attempting to create acceptable assessment plans while the threat of losing accreditation hung in the balance. Many university administrators comforted themselves with the belief that assessment was just another fad and would blow over by the time of the next accreditation visit. The plans that were created were largely one dimensional and limited to classroom-level assessment, or they were broad-stroked university-level assessment based upon existing data, irregular data collection, and convenience samples. While potentially useful data may have been collected, it was seldom used in a way to help the institution improve.

It has since become apparent that assessment, as demanded by regional and professional accrediting bodies (not to mention the public, granting agencies, and various elected public officials), is not going away. In fact, the emphasis on assessment has gained momentum; and effective assessment needs to be part of a comprehensive, institution-wide plan for all educational levels, which should include all academic and nonacademic departments, programs, and units.

Foundations for Effective Assessment Programs

For assessment programs to be effective, those involved must first recognize the value of assessment. Next, the core values of the institution must be assessed and understood. Finally, effective assessment programs must have visionary leadership. Without these critical elements, such programs cannot succeed.

Recognition of the value of assessment. Assessment provides an opportunity for an institution to learn about itself through student performance outcomes. This self-reflective knowledge adds value for students, faculty, and the institution.

Assessment can provide students with information comparing their performance to others in their class, others in their respective states, others in the nation, or a set of identified performance criteria. Formative (or process-level) assessment data can help students get back on track if they have strayed from their academic goals, or it can reaffirm excellent performance. Process-level assessment can include criterion-based grades on an assignment, pretests (PSATs), midterm student conferences, or review of student portfolios.

Summative (or results-level) assessment of student performance provides evidence of what the student has accomplished and what goals require additional work following graduation. College entrance exams, placement tests, regent's exams, proficiency tests, and refereed performances all provide summative evidence of student accomplishments. Additionally, students who have collected assessment data in portfolios throughout their educational experiences have powerful summative evidence of their learning to present to potential employers or to institutions where they are applying for further education.

If structured appropriately, every assessment experience provides students with timely feedback and direction for self-improvement, along with incentives to continue to participate seriously in assessment efforts. Assessment programs at any level will derail quickly if student participants never receive personal feedback or never learn the collective results of the assessment exercise.

Assessment provides educators with direction on how to facilitate learning. By constantly monitoring student performance in their classes and programs, faculty are able to determine which teaching methods and content impact students most positively. By maintaining contact with the next education level (elementary school to high school, high school to college, college to graduate school) and employers, faculty are able to assesses how well curricula and programs are preparing students for future endeavors. Teachers dedicated to assessment engage in continuous revision of courses, curricula, and programs that is based upon assessment data; such revision creates exciting, relevant, and effective learning opportunities for students.

Institutions that effectively engage in formative and summative assessment of student performance will be able to deliver a world-class education to their students. These institutions will have confidence that every student they graduate will possess the knowledge, skills, and values of an educated person, one who is prepared to meet the needs of the new century workplace. Concerted attention to student performance, compounded with appropriate interventions and timely innovations, allows institutions to respond conscientiously to concerns. Student retention, satisfaction, and success are all enhanced through assessment.

Assessing the core values. The fundamental role of assessment is to *measure what is valued.* In order to capture the collective imagination and energy of the institution, assessment must be seen as practical, relevant, and grounded in the identity of the institution. Statements about student outcomes at this level are likely to be broad and general.

As Banta, Lund, Black, and Oblander (1996) explain,

> *Assessment has the greatest chance for success when it is based on educational values. This means that for assessment to be truly effective—from an institutional perspective—in improving that which is important, institutional agents including trustees, administrators, faculty, staff, students, and outside publics must first have a*

*shared conception as to what the institution is, what it values, and
what it aspires to be. This is not an easy task, for there is perhaps
no more important, nor difficult, undertaking. (p. 4)*

Assessment should measure performance and progress made toward the
achievement of the educational goals of a particular institution. It should begin
with what the institution values and how the institution envisions itself. Assessment becomes the yardstick by which progress and alignment can be measured
and how the institution positions itself relative to other similar institutions. But
assessment is not just about measurement, it is about interpreting the measures
and making changes to close the gaps between the current situation and desired
goal.

Visionary leadership. Effective assessment requires a passionate commitment on the part of an institution's educational leaders. The dedication must be
shared by many, but led by a charismatic visionary who understands assessment
as more than a collection of statistical techniques and methodologies. This
individual must be daring, bold, and creative in his or her approach to assessment.

The visionary must possess specialized analytical skills and system
expertise for success. Empirical investigation is important when exploring the
complex issues that assessment must address. But the visionary knows that
assessment is more than measuring for statistical inconsistencies. He or she
understands that assessment is measuring the performance of real people and
respects the "humanistic" side of assessment as much as the statistical side.

To the visionary, assessment is an exploration of the process and product
of learning. Peters and Austin (1985) discuss the importance of the visionary
leader in an educational system's assessment efforts as follows:

*There is no magic: only people who find and nurture champions,
dramatize ... goals and direction, build skills and teams, spread
irresistible enthusiasm. They are cheerleaders, coaches, storytell-
ers, and wanderers. They encourage, excite, teach, listen, facilitate.
Their actions are consistent. You know they take their priorities
seriously because they live them clearly and visibly. They walk the
talk. (pp. 282-283)*

The visionary does not seek or expect answers, but, instead, understands
that assessment has multiple layers and realizes that peeling back one layer
reveals new and increasingly engaging questions. To this individual, evidence
worthy of analysis is everywhere. The visionary is part detective, explorer,
archaeologist, psychologist, and evangelist. Without a visionary assessment
leader, efforts are not likely to capture the imagination of faculty or students and
are destined to remain in the mechanical model of the past.

Assessment: The Present and the Future

To transform assessment from a required exercise to an important and genuinely useful part of an institution's culture, assessment in the new century will need to be driven by new and different theories and methodologies than those currently utilized.

Leadership. Assessment is too often the sole responsibility of central administration. While support of assessment at the administrative level is essential, successful assessment programs must be faculty-driven, not administrator-driven. Faculty must embrace assessment for how it can provide information that can improve teaching and learning. This will require them to shift their focus away from thinking about assessment as a remote testing and evaluation exercise. They must recognize that they have the power and responsibility to assess, adapt, and innovate the classroom, curriculum, and program levels to maximize student learning.

Implementation. A broad range of tools can be used to assess student learning. Commercially or locally developed surveys and tests are the cornerstone of most school assessment programs. These instruments, when used over time, provide a baseline from which the institution can monitor progress or compare itself to national norms. However, there is an inherent danger in locking into specific tools or methodologies, as they can limit the institution's vision and horizon, to say nothing of the temptation of teaching to the test.

Effective assessment must be needs-driven, not survey-driven. Assessment activities need to be cumulative, building on each other, shaped by previously gained knowledge. The menu of assessment techniques and methods that an institution utilizes needs to be both fluid and dynamic. While the state may mandate specific instruments, it is up to schools and institutions to personalize their assessment efforts by using these instruments in combination with their own school-specific assessment tools.

Additionally, as new questions arise, new techniques and methods are required. In assessment, there are no wrong answers, only questions that go unanswered because schools are locked into historically and externally mandated methodologies and tools without regard to how the data will shape knowledge. They become locked into comparing themselves against the past or other institutions instead of positioning themselves for the future and the good of their students.

Data collection. Educational institutions have access to a lot of data. Unfortunately, much of the data collected (especially through normed surveys and tests) is never used in any meaningful, reflective way. Though system offices will express the need for national comparative data, this data is seldom used except for occasional publicity purposes. It rarely facilitates change.

Institutions undertaking a serious assessment initiative should start with an examination of every piece of information that is known about their institutions and examine every piece of data for its potential utility. If the question is irrelevant, if it provides no clear information, if it does not help institutions understand their students, or if it has no foreseeable use as an independent or dependent variable, then collecting it is a waste of time. Most institutions would make great strides in assessment by starting with creating their own assessment instruments rather than continuing to be both overwhelmed and limited by standardized data collection tools.

Data storage. The inability to store data efficiently and effectively is probably the biggest limitation to most current educational assessment programs. Data is usually stored in collection silos or warehouses, a separate one for each type of data (satisfaction data, subject matter examinations, graduating senior surveys, etc.). These silos are often located in different places throughout the educational institution and have no interconnectivity. Often, there is a lack of universal data collection standards.

Additionally, technical problems arise as databases come online at different times. Data provided on disk from various testing and survey organizations creates additional silos. The result is that the data cannot be linked to other data. Relationships go unexplored.

It is in these relationships, however, that the real knowledge about student behavior and performance can be found. Effective assessment is relationship-driven and is essentially an exploration of the dynamic relationships among data. Isolating the data limits the ability to learn from it. Universal data collection standards need to be developed with centralized databases. A robust analytical tool would help identify the relationships and highlight the areas most in need of change.

Context. Current assessment wisdom and practice promote the analysis of student cohorts against each other or benchmarks—for example, first-year students compared to seniors or current data compared to data from three years ago. Though often collected in a systematic, efficient manner, the data has limited utility because it is removed from the individual student. In efforts to maintain the integrity of the data by preserving the anonymity of the respondents, the richness of the data has been lost.

Assessment needs to be student-driven, not cohort-group-driven. Data needs to be interpreted in relation to each student's background and goals. Again, it is the relationship between the student and the data that creates the knowledge. No knowledge is inherent in the data itself—knowledge can only come from the interpretation of the data in relation to the goals and background of individuals.

Timing. At most schools, assessment happens on specific days during certain times of the year. Days set aside for standardized testing are common in K–12 classrooms; assessment days are also becoming increasingly common in colleges and universities. If used correctly, these assessment times serve as a powerful cultural symbol of an institution's commitment to assessment. Assessment days give institutions the chance to take stock of their situation. Conducted over successive years, assessment days provide a benchmark from which to measure progress.

However, this approach also compartmentalizes assessment by separating it from the ongoing institutional activities. It isolates instead of integrates assessment into the institution's ongoing culture. When it only happens on a couple of days a year, it can easily be ignored. Effective assessment is demand-driven, not convenience-driven. Successful assessment programs in both K–12 and higher education classrooms are ongoing, continuous, and fully integrated into the day-to-day business of the institution. Activities are timed to fit a student's experience, not the school calendar.

Accreditation. Perhaps the biggest push for assessment has come from the agencies that accredit our nation's schools. While the threat of losing accreditation adds urgency and some credibility to assessment, the reality is that very few assessment programs do not ebb and flow with accreditation cycles.

The pressure of mandated assessment is a mixed blessing. On the one hand, it has forced schools to take assessment of student learning seriously. On the other hand, the accreditation mandates have promoted sterile, mechanistic approaches to assessment. This is most clearly seen in the creation of "one-size-fits-all" standardized tests and graduation standards. These approaches generate little enthusiasm or excitement for assessment. Assessment becomes a bland exercise in filling out forms and checking off requirements instead of a process that engages an institution's collective energy, creativity, and imagination.

Assessment programs that consist of sporadic bursts of assessment activity in the months prior to the self-study visit are usually followed by a collective sigh of relief and a return to business as usual following the accreditation review. There is no systematic improvement as a result of the data collected.

Assessment needs to be improvement-driven, not accreditation-driven. It will only capture the enthusiasm of an institution if it is seen as a genuine, sincere effort to improve through continual analysis, discussion, and innovation. Without a clear and public feedback loop, assessment will be a continuous uphill battle in which no one emerges better for the effort.

Summary

From its early psychological and military applications, assessment has evolved to become an integral part of the culture of educational institutions across the country. Assessment is being promoted by legislators, leveraged by accrediting bodies, and demanded by the public. Elementary and secondary schools, postsecondary institutions, and colleges/universities are becoming increasingly involved in the assessment process with the goals of increasing accountability and improving the quality of our nation's educational outcomes. Educational institutions have responded with an array of theories and approaches to assessment, linking assessment results to everything from graduation standards to performance-based funding.

For institutions to have effective assessment programs, the assessment process must be valued, the institution's core values must be understood, and the programs need to have visionary leadership. The journey toward continuous improvement based upon assessment results helps educational institutions to become more accountable for learning experiences and the expected outcomes related to those experiences. Sound assessment programs enable institutions to become self-monitoring, self-correcting, and self-regarding.

The new millennium presents unprecedented opportunities for educational institutions to challenge themselves and to aspire toward heretofore unimagined and hence unrealized goals by using assessment for the good of the institution, the community, and most importantly, the students served.

References

Astin, A. W. (1993). *What matters in college? Four critical years revisited.* San Francisco: Jossey-Bass Inc., Publishers.

Banta, T. W., Lund, J. P., Black, K., & Oblander F. W. (Eds.). (1996). *Assessment in practice: Putting principles to work on college campuses.* San Francisco: Jossey-Bass Inc., Publishers.

Hartle, T. W. (1986). The growing interest in measuring the educational achievement of college students. *Assessment in American higher education: Issues and contexts.* Washington, DC: Office of Educational Research and Improvement, U.S. Department of Education. (ED 260 676)

Marchese, T. (1993). TQM: A time for ideas. *Change, 25,* 10–13.

Peters, T., & Austin, N. (1985). *A passion for excellence: The leadership difference.* New York: Warner Books.

Peterson, R. O. (1999). Creating a context to support assessment. In *A collection of papers on self-study and institutional improvement: 1999 edition.* Chicago: North Central Association of Colleges and Schools, Commission on Institutions of Higher Education.

Stiggins, R. J. (1994). *Student-centered assessment.* New York: Macmillan College Publishing Company.

The Importance of Assessment in Business Education

Sandy Braathen and Marcel Robles
University of North Dakota
Grand Forks, North Dakota

Starting in the 1970s and continuing through the 1980s, Americans began scrutinizing public education more closely, calling for changes to enhance its quality. With the education reform movement came new ways of looking at the teaching and learning process, increased accountability for student learning outcomes, and a new emphasis on both program and student assessment.

Throughout the 1990s continued emphasis has been placed on assessment. Many articles and books examine why assessment is needed and how to improve it. According to Roeber (1996),

> *Student assessment is viewed nationally as the pivotal piece around which school reform and improvement in the nation's schools turn. For example, student assessment is the key piece of Goals 2000, as well as other federal legislation such as the Elementary and Secondary Education Act (ESEA). (p. 3)*

Rabinowitz (1995) echoes this sentiment when he discusses how both the Goals 2000 and the School-to-Work Opportunities Act emphasize high standards while preparing students for the workplace. He stresses the importance of developing flexible assessment systems in order to be more accountable both to the government and to the students served. As a result of school reform, Roeber (1996) believes more and more assessment, often using novel techniques, will occur in both traditionally and nontraditionally assessed areas in our schools. "Collectively, these standards represent substantial challenges for the American schools. They imply that all students will need to achieve at much higher levels.

New strategies for assessment are also implied by these content standards" (Roeber, 1996, p. 3).

In addition to the ESEA discussed by Roeber, another significant piece of legislation is the 1998 Perkins Act, which increases the necessity for assessment over that outlined in the 1990 Perkins Act. The 1990 Act required educators to conduct annual program evaluations. The intent of the legislation was to use performance information to "evaluate and improve secondary and postsecondary offerings" (Hoachlander, 1995, p. 21). The 1998 Perkins Act "presents new opportunities for states to show the impact of vocational education programs," but it also increases the burden of student follow-up (Hettinger, 1999).

The 1998 Perkins Act requires states to set performance levels for four categories or core indicators: student attainment of skill proficiencies; acquisition of degrees or credentials; placement and retention in postsecondary education or employment; and completion of programs leading to nontraditional training and employment. Performance levels for these categories must be reported in "percentages or numbers to make sure they are 'objective, quantifiable, and measurable' the law says" (Hettinger, 1999, p. 41).

Increased or improved assessment typically has been the answer to increased pressure from the public. More than ever, business educators are concerned about proving the quality of education and of business education programs. Assessments can provide the vehicle to validate business education programs as well as document business education students' learning outcomes.

Legislative or even state mandates are not the only reasons to conduct assessment. Business educators can gain a wealth of useful information by conducting assessments and by actively participating in the assessment process. Rather than simply allowing administrators to collect required numbers and forward them to state officials, business teachers need to be active participants. Educators must realize that the information gathered can be used to better manage and improve programs (Hoachlander, 1995; Roeber, 1996).

Rather than viewing assessment as something done to teachers or as something done to students, business educators need to view it as a vital component of effective instruction. According to the Policies Commission for Business and Economic Education's (PCBEE) Statement No. 59 (1996): "Integral to instruction, assessment is the continuing process of teachers and students engaged in the review, critique, and evaluation of student actions and accomplishments." The end results of assessment should include measurable standards and student motivation to improve performance.

Additionally, while educational reform has called for a more integrated curriculum, business educators have realized a need to demonstrate that their curricula meet high standards. Kerka (1995) believes that authentic assessment meets both needs because it joins the assessment from the workplace and the school. "It focuses on tasks that are meaningful to learners and linked to school and nonschool demands" (Kerka, p. 3).

Assessment should involve a mix of techniques and strategies that give each student the opportunity to work at his or her individual pace and reach his or her fullest potential. As each student develops a philosophy of assessment in business education, business educators need to formulate their own questions:

- What knowledge is the student learning today?
- How is the learning taking place?
- What is the role of the teacher in the classroom?
- What are the objectives of today's lesson?
- What, if any, concepts should be evaluated or assessed?
- Will today's lesson objectives carry through to students' personal and professional lives?

Assessment and Accountability in Business Education

As a result of the many reform efforts, educational institutions must strive to produce the highest possible quality of student learning (Angelo and Cross, 1993). There is increased demand for accountability from parents, students, employers, and administrators. Across the board, there is a push to adopt assessment programs that will assist with measuring student learning and improving instructional programs. Widespread agreement exists that assessment data should be used to document and improve student performance while also integrating learning goals and outcomes (Giddings, Boles, and Cloud, 1996).

The PCBEE Statement No. 59 emphasizes the assessment of student achievement in business education in order to hold business educators account-able for what students know and are able to accomplish. Business education curriculum and teaching methods should be responsive to both student and societal needs. As the needs change, business education should evolve to meet those needs (Sanstead, 1993).

In addition, legislation like the 1998 Perkins Act has called for increased accountability. Educators need to prove the effectiveness of their programs more than ever. Neils Brooks, Virginia's vocational education director, discusses how federal funding will be tied to student achievement. He welcomes the increased accountability because it also brings increased flexibility: "I don't know any situation where you can have flexibility without accountability" (cited in Hettinger, 1999, p 42).

When assessment is combined with the teaching and learning process, it helps to provide the accountability for both the learner and the educational institution (Pearce and Hess, 1999). Giddings, Boles, and Cloud (1996) note that assessment has been credited with promoting critical thinking in education, demonstrating accountability to the public, and giving credibility to the educational institution.

The PCBEE Statement No. 62 (1998) states that multiple formal and informal assessment techniques should be used to measure achievement of standards in business teacher education as well. Once it became widely recognized that teachers were "at the heart" of education, it became clear that educational reform needed to begin with the reform of teacher education.

In the 1980s a greater emphasis was placed on higher teacher standards. In order to be credentialed, teachers were required to demonstrate their knowledge and skills in actual teaching situations (Lyons, 1998). Assessment continues to be viewed as a requirement of excellent teaching. Teachers must reflect upon their instructional methodologies and adapt their teaching strategies as they refine their curricula; this requires constant enhancement of knowledge and improvement of teaching approaches.

If, as PCBEE No. 62 states, "business teacher educators are accountable for the preparation of teachers who can meet the instructional needs of all students," there is a continuous loop of passing the legacy of assessment on to the next generation of business education teachers.

Assessment of Teaching and Learning Effectiveness

Along with school reform comes new ways of assessing students. "Assessment is important because it is widely believed that what gets assessed is what gets taught, and the format of assessment influences the format of learning and teaching" (Roeber, 1996, p. 3).

In order for assessment to enhance teaching and learning, it must be an ongoing process to which all participants are committed. Classroom assessment is particularly useful for determining how well students are learning at each milestone and for providing information for improvement when learning is less than satisfactory (Angelo and Cross, 1993). By practicing assessment in the classroom, teachers will become better able to understand and promote learning and increase their ability to help students become more effective, self-assessing, and self-directed learners (Angelo and Cross, 1993). Assessment should be viewed as a means to provide the data and analysis needed for continuous improvement. "We must be better at collecting evidence that goals and objectives are being met. Narrow standards will only produce narrow results" (Hanson and Teeter, 1995, p. 43).

Designing effective assessment. Since the curriculum has changed, teachers also need to change the ways they demonstrate teaching and learning effectiveness (Hanson and Teeter, 1995). Assessment instruments should be designed to provide students with feedback and help them to understand and apply what they have learned. They need to see the "fit" of the material with a real-world application. Pedagogically, students begin to understand that learning can occur in collective contexts, whereby they learn what they can also contribute to the group (Weimer, 1999).

Nationally, standardized testing with its "fill-in-the-bubble" mentality has proliferated. The public has demanded more rigorous and visible accountability. They want to know what and how well students are learning. A simplistic answer is to create more tests; however, other voices are being heard. Educators are advocating for "authentic assessment"—real evidence of real learning—which is currently a desirable and worthwhile curriculum innovation. Genuine enthusiasm exists for measuring the varied kinds of learning we teach and that we hope will occur. This has been very helpful for educators since it has focused instruction upon student learning and outcomes. We have had to review, analyze, and reject things we have done previously, perhaps routinely and conventionally, without real commitment (Hanson and Teeter, 1995, p. 41).

More than a series of standardized tests or even end-of-the-term exams is required. Such tests are not measures of assessment, but rather evaluation tools for assigning grades. Many times the test score does not reflect the student's knowledge of the material. Hanson and Teeter (1995) state that paper-and-pencil tests simply do not fully measure learning outcomes (especially tests with only one right answer). "Assessment that becomes too technical and too objective will ignore and negate the creative, the interpretive and analytical, and the unique expressions of the student" (Hanson and Teeter, 1995, p. 42).

A second trap to avoid is testing students on subject matter not taught, which frustrates students and gives the teacher inaccurate testing results. This is typically a result of not aligning testing with the objectives and the subject matter. The objectives need to be clearly identified and the assessment tools must reflect the learning desired.

For any assessment system developed, the following principles should be followed to help ensure success:

- Clear and concise standards should be identified;
- A variety of assessment measures should be used;
- Assessment tasks should be primarily performance-based and developed jointly by educators and industry representatives;
- The end result of assessment should be "artifacts that can be scored at a later time and accumulated in a working folder or portfolio"; and
- Equity concerns must be addressed throughout the assessment process (Rabinowitz, 1995).

Active and authentic assessment. Effective assessment needs to be both active and authentic. Active assessment "offers different methods that require students to demonstrate competencies or knowledge by creating a solution or product. These methods range from simple student-constructed responses to comprehensive demonstrations or collections of large pieces of work over time. Such active assessments aim to provide problem-solving situations for students to demonstrate application of relevant skills and knowledge" (Pearce and Hess, 1999, p. 7).

Authentic assessment "involves measuring students' performances in more natural, real-world settings rather than in artificial, contrived settings typically found in standardized testing protocols" (Block; Lieberman, and Connor-Kuntz, 1998, p. 49). With authentic assessment, there is a link between the outcomes the teacher has determined to be relevant and important and those outcomes the student has determined to be relevant and important. Rather than giving a student a single test, authentic assessment aims to provide a more comprehensive look at what the student is able to accomplish, using the learned skills and knowledge.

The basic definitions and characteristics of authentic assessment developed by Block, Lieberman, and Connor-Kuntz (1998) are relevant to any field, including business education. They identify six basic characteristics of authentic assessment:

1. Choosing tasks based on real-world requirements. Teachers use situations that the student would experience in the real world rather than contrived situations. Zeliff and Schultz (1998) provide the example of desktop publishing students preparing the printed programs for a music concert. "The students gather information, design a layout, key information, and print a draft copy. After the music director reviews the draft copy, desired changes are made, and a final copy is printed. The finished product is then distributed at the concert" (pp. 1-2).

2. Having students apply higher-level thinking and concepts. Such exercises measure "students' abilities to think and to apply general concepts to a variety of situations" (Block, Lieberman, and Connor-Kuntz, 1998, p. 49). Teachers give students a variety of situations or multiple conditions in which to apply what they have learned to solve the problems or demonstrate competence. Zeliff and Schultz (1998) provide an example of this characteristic: "Statistics of sports teams entered into a spreadsheet or database is a realistic application of students' computer application skills. Results can be prepared for the coaches and teams as graphs, charts, or reports" (p. 2).

3. Articulating criteria in advance. Students know ahead of time what they will be working on and what constitutes mastery. This provides the capability for assessment information to "be used to guide improvement throughout the learning process" (Block, Lieberman, and Connor-Kuntz, 1998, p. 49).

4. Making assessment part of the curriculum. Rather than simply conducting assessments at the end of the unit or semester, authentic assessment "is linked directly to the curriculum and instruction so that the teacher and students can make adjustments during the unit" (Block, Lieberman, and Connor-Kuntz, 1998, p. 50).

5. Having students present work publicly. "One of the hallmarks of authentic assessment is public performance ... Again, the best types of public performance occur in real-life settings rather than under contrived testing situations" (Block, Lieberman, and Connor-Kuntz, 1998, p. 50). Allowing students to perform in "real" settings is the best way to have them demonstrate their skill and knowledge levels. Zeliff and Schultz (1998) provide the Volunteer Income Tax Assistance (VITA) program as a good example of public performance. In this program, college students prepare income tax statements for elderly citizens. The program is typically sponsored jointly by the IRS and collegiate accounting programs.

6. Demonstrating student competence in a variety of situations. "Finally, authentic assessment is characterized by performance in many situations and settings rather than in one test situation" (Block, Lieberman, and Connor-Kuntz, 1998, p. 50).

Types of assessment. Zeliff and Schultz (1998) identify three types of assessment used to provide feedback for students in business education: traditional, alternative, and performance. Traditional assessment typically measures lower-level cognitive skills. This domain includes factual recall and comprehension. Alternative assessment measures the affective domain and includes team activities, evaluations of self and peers, and reflection through logs and portfolios. This type of assessment examines students' attitudes and character traits. Performance assessment measures the psychomotor domain and includes students' demonstrations of competence in a skill or task. Examples include formatting documents, completing financial statements, and transcribing dictation.

An effective teacher will always find ways to demonstrate that learning has occurred. One method alone will not be enough to measure all of the objectives and outcomes desired. For assessment to be effective, educators need to expand the assessment measures they use. Roeber (1996) lists a variety of assessment techniques available: short-answer questions, extended-response questions, individual interviews, performance events, performance tasks in which students have extended time, projects, portfolios, observations, anecdotal records, and multiple-choice exercises.

Another approach to varied methods is the three p's of student performance: performance tasks, projects, and portfolios (Hanson and Teeter, 1995). This approach requires that the performance tasks be clearly identified and articulated. When a student completes a final project, it is a tangible example of the student's learning outcomes. With a portfolio, students make selections of their own work as evidence of learning.

Development of student portfolios can be an excellent performance indicator of student learning. Portfolios allow students to reflect upon what has been learned and how the learning fits into the curriculum. The curriculum should be designed so that it focuses on learning, and students can integrate their portfolios to track both what they are learning and how they are learning it (Angelo and Cross, 1993; Weimer, 1999). The portfolio concept can provide a rich, qualitative alternative during the assessment process, as opposed to using a quantitative approach to student evaluation rating data (Weimer, 1999). Portfolios can be a compilation of all active assessment measures, such as checklists, self-reflections, process pieces, and performances. These measures encourage the learner to develop a visual representation of self-reflected artifacts, teaching competencies, and a holistic view of teaching philosophy (Pearce and Hess, 1999).

Checklists and rubrics, "detailed guidelines for making scoring decisions" (Block, Lieberman, and Connor-Kuntz, 1998, p. 50), are tools that will help involve students in their own self-evaluation while giving them a guide for their performance. Rubrics have specific scoring criteria and standards for various levels of performance or gradations of quality. By providing students with a clearer sense of the expectations, checklists and rubrics lead to improved products produced by the students.

Another form of assessment involves the use of group activities. Such activities allow students to discuss the answers to questions and to synthesize the course content covered during the class period. As a group, they indicate a consensus as to the understanding of the material. If one member does not feel that he or she comprehends the concepts, the other group members help explain it. Not only do students assess their own learning, but they also improve upon that learning by reinforcing the newfound knowledge. The instructor, in turn, receives relevant feedback about student comprehension of the material (Jackson Hester, 1998).

Traditionally, assessment has been viewed as a process to be conducted at the end (end of unit, end of semester or grading period, completion of a program, graduation and matriculation, etc.). However, assessment provides teachers with a means to examine the impact of their instructional strategies on a daily basis as well. Many times gaps exist between what was taught and what has been learned, and, by the time the teacher notices these gaps in understanding, it is frequently too late to remedy the problems (Angelo and Cross, 1993). Assessment can give the teacher feedback on the effectiveness of that day's teaching method. The teacher then self-reflects on how well the students learned the material as a result of the instructional method.

Assessment can also help students to become more actively engaged in the learning process. Students need to develop the ability to continually assess their knowledge and build upon that knowledge as they incorporate new ideas and information. When they are aware of their present level of knowledge, students are also more comfortable making the transition to the next level.

Developing assessment systems. According to Rabinowitz (1995), the first step in creating an assessment system is to determine the purpose of the assessment. "The key to developing a true system of assessment is to get a handle on what actually needs to be measured. The number of potential purposes of assessment are as varied as the instruments" (p. 28). When developing a new assessment system, it is helpful to look to others for advice. What has been done in similar programs? What assistance might be available (from administration at local or state levels)?

Both validity and reliability must be considered when designing assessment instruments. The information being sought needs to be clearly defined and the instrument needs to be representative of the information desired. Other factors to consider are time involved, cost, and ease of use. Attending workshops or other special presentations can also be helpful (Giddings, Boles, and Cloud, 1996).

"A primary concern when beginning an assessment program is who will be responsible for implementing and reporting on the process" (Giddings, Boles, and Cloud, 1996, p. 230). Again, regardless of ultimate responsibility, all participants need to be actively involved in the process in order for it to be effective. Any discussions on program effectiveness should be collaborative, and decisions regarding change should be made collectively.

"The information gained from assessment can be used to guide the design of strategies for improving instruction, advising, faculty-student interactions, and other activities that affect program effectiveness and student development" (Vandament, 1987, cited in Giddings, Boles, and Cloud, 1996, p. 232).

The assessment process followed by the Southern Regional Education Board (SREB) consortium members, for example, involves five essential features: goal setting, key practices and strategies, benchmarking, self-assessment, and planning and implementing program improvement.

Goal setting involves the effective use of goals and objectives, which need to be preestablished and based on clear and concise standards.

Key practices and strategies need to be carefully considered and thoughtfully implemented. A variety of assessment techniques should be used to monitor students or outcomes. In addition, to enhance programs, consideration of the effectiveness of the practices or strategies used should also be considered. When making changes to the key practices or strategies, instructors need to monitor the progress on implementing the changes.

Benchmarking should be used along with goal setting. "Benchmarks are different from goals in that they represent real achievements" (Hoachlander, 1995, p. 22). A benchmark is something that has already been attained and can be more realistic than a goal. An example would be looking at what similar programs have achieved and then selecting the highest level for a particular program's benchmark. Key variables for similarity include "size, geographic location (urban, suburban, rural), percentage of students with special needs or expenditures per student" (Hoachlander, 1995, p. 22). There is no one right way to pick a benchmark.

Self-assessment should be an integral part of the assessment process. Educators need to compare their program's performance on key outcome measures with the selected benchmarks. Hoachlander (1995) emphasizes the importance of widespread participation in the assessment. It should not just be conducted by administrators. Rather, "it should first involve faculty, counselors, and other staff who are in the best position to understand why particular results are occurring and what changes in curriculum, teaching practices, and student services and other aspects of daily operations might yield better performance" (Hoachlander, 1995, p. 50). Teachers, counselors, and other staff need to be involved in review and interpretation of data, group discussion and planning, and goal and performance objective setting.

Planning and implementing program improvement should be an ongoing part of the assessment process. A program improvement plan should consist of a current status report, strategies to be used to improve performance, and objectives for progressing toward goals. The quantitative data gathered needs to be supplemented with personal judgment, common sense, and additional qualitative assessments (Hoachlander, 1995).

Assessment of Student Performance

In any business education program, every student's level of performance should reflect the knowledge and competencies necessary for success in the business environment and in everyday life. Assessment should address the skills required of students, the amount of student involvement in their own learning, the standards, and the feedback to students about their progress towards their goals.

Assessing student performance for success in business. The demands of today's business world require students to be competent in the business education fields. This is true whether they are performing accounting functions, using a computer, or participating in an entrepreneurship class. "The workplace today has embraced new technologies, management philosophies, and organizational structures. Today's workers use computers, work in teams, and assist in management decisions" (Zeliff and Schultz, 1998, p. 1).

Employers want employees with critical thinking skills, teamwork orientation, self-regulatory skills, adaptability, and flexibility; and "they want meaningful evidence of these capacities in potential employees" (Kerka, 1995, p. 3). "To prepare students for this changing workplace, business educators must use a variety of learning activities and provide feedback to foster student development of these new skills, attitudes, and knowledge" (Zeliff and Schultz, 1998, p. 1).

To help prepare students for working in "the real world" of business, educators need to develop an assessment system that is flexible and "developed with input from employers, that measures academic, job readiness, and technical skills in a meaningful way" (Rabinowitz, 1995, p. 27). By providing assessment systems that meet the needs of business and industry, business educators can emphasize the value of business education programs.

As previously discussed, adding flexibility to assessment systems would allow for project and portfolio approaches to complement the traditional paper-and-pencil testing approaches. Students who develop portfolios prepare for employment in business because they follow the same process as many performance appraisals used in business organizations. Assessment also helps students to demonstrate verbal and written communication skills, exhibit problem-solving and decision-making skills, and become aware of the diversity of people in the global business environment. Students make better use of technology, as well as collaborative and leadership skills. Teamwork and group discussion give students the opportunity to communicate and participate as they would on a project team in the business world. Learners gain insight on how to approach problem solving and analysis.

. **Assessing student performance for success in life.** Regardless of the careers they pursue, individuals will be using business technology to obtain and keep their jobs. As part of the everyday life of being a consumer, students need to know how to balance a checkbook, calculate loan payments, use a computer, type a research paper, prepare a résumé, complete a job application, and participate in the interview process. Students need to know how to use technology for communication by electronic mail, voice mail, facsimile, or other means.

Hanson and Teeter (1995) cite Howard Gardner (1988) in discussing the deficiencies of traditional assessment. "Testing ... is a school phenomenon, peculiar to classroom learning. Once you leave school you may never take another test. However, in real life, we find continual purpose in using the skills and knowledge we should have learned in school" (p. 41).

Pearce and Hess (1999) believe assessment practices need to "engage the learner in performing the life tasks of solving problems, collaborating with others, applying knowledge, and using learning strategies" (p. 12). Beaudry and Schaub (1998) state that teaching students to think critically about connections between characters and events in classroom subject matter and in their own lives is necessary. Students should formulate questions as they learn new knowledge and apply that knowledge to their lives.

Learners should be involved in self-assessment. Self-reflection requires students to examine the intrapersonal learning experience by promoting under-standing of conceptual knowledge and application for problem-solving in the real world (Pearce and Hess, 1999). "Moments of reflection and self-analysis are necessary for growth and development in all areas of life" (Jackson Hester, 1998, p. 2).

Throughout the assessment process, it is important to remember that learning is a social process that allows individuals to grow as members of a lifelong learning community. Intrinsic motivation makes the learning challenge meaningful to the individual (Pearson and Hess, 1999). Assessment is a holistic approach to addressing the total curriculum and integration of the learning experiences that occur in and out of the classroom. The more the concept applies to the external environment, the more relevant and meaningful it will be for the student.

Summary

Assessment is an integral part of effective teaching and quality student learning; and with public education being scrutinized so closely today, it is more important than ever before. Educational reform, high standards, and the demand for accountability increase the need for assessment to demonstrate student achievement and performance. As schools become more involved in assessing student outcomes, information is needed about what assessment is and how it can be accomplished. Assessment may be performed at the institutional level, at the program level, or specifically within the classroom.

A comprehensive assessment program will include a variety of strategies to measure student performance. Several studies have reported assessment within various programs using many different techniques. Key considerations in assessing the effectiveness of teaching and learning include the strategic design of the assessment instrument, the utilization of both active and authentic assess-ment, the most appropriate type of assessment strategy for the subject matter, and the development of the assessment system.

Not only will assessment prove beneficial in determining how to improve business education effectiveness, but also this improvement will enhance the viability of the business education program. The business education teacher should use the results of the performance measurement continually to revise curriculum and instructional strategies. Schools involved in assessment report that teachers have developed greater interest in students and the teaching and learning process, and that faculty members interact more with their colleagues as a result of the need to reach consensus on assessment goals and activities (Vandament, 1987, cited in Giddings, Boles, and Cloud, 1996). Halpern (1987, cited in Giddings, Boles, and Cloud, 1996) affirms that assessment provides a more effective method for improving student learning and for evaluating the effects of actions to accomplish improvement.

Used effectively, assessment can benefit students, teachers, employers, the business education program, and the educational institution; it can validate student competency for work in the business world or for everyday life. As new assessment strategies continue to emerge, their impact will be profound, affecting not only students and teachers, but also schools and their basic organizational structure.

References

American Vocational Association. (1998). Comparison of the 1990 and 1998 Perkins Acts. In *The official guide to the Perkins Act of 1998*. Reston, VA: American Vocational Association.

Angelo, T. A., & Cross, K. P. (1993). *Classroom assessment techniques: A handbook for college teachers* (2nd ed.). San Francisco: Jossey-Bass Inc., Publishers.

Beaudry, M. L., & Schaub, T. (1998). The learning-centered syllabus. *The Teaching Professor, 12* (2), 1–2.

Block, M. E., Lieberman, L. J., & Connor-Kuntz, F. (1998). Authentic assessment in adapted physical education. *The Journal of Physical Education, Recreation, and Dance, 69* (3), 48–55.

Giddings, V. L., Boles, J. F., & Cloud, R. M. (1996). Assessment: Practices and implications for home economics in higher education. *Family and Consumer Sciences Research Journal, 24* (3), 219.

Hanson, J. M., & Teeter, L. (1995). Assessment in art. *School Arts, 94* (6), 41–43.

Hettinger, J. (1999). The new Perkins ... finally. *Techniques, 73,* 40–42.

Hoachlander, G. (1995). What the numbers really mean. *Vocational Education Journal, 70* (3), 20–23, 50.

Jackson Hester, E. (1998). Taking meta-cognitive moments. *The Teaching Professor, 12* (2), 2.

Kerka, S. (1995). *Authentic assessment in vocational education. Trends and issue alerts.* Sponsored by the Office of Educational Research and Improvement, Columbus, OH: ERIC Clearinghouse on Adult, Career, and Vocational Education. (ERIC Document Reproduction Service No. ED 384 736)

Lyons, N. (Ed.). (1998). *With portfolio in hand: Validating the new teacher professionalism*. New York: Teachers College Press.

Pearce, K., & Hess, C. (1999). Constructivism and assessment. *Faculty Development—The Collaboration for the Advancement of College Teaching and Learning, 12* (2), 6–8, 12.

Policies Commission for Business and Economic Education (PCBEE). (1996, October). Statement 59: This we believe about assessing student achievement in business education. *Business Education Forum, 49* (1), 20–21.

Policies Commission for Business and Economic Education (PCBEE). (1998, October). Statement 62: This we believe about the role of standards for business education. *Business Education Forum, 53* (1), 20–21.

Policies Commission for Business and Economic Education (PCBEE). (1998, October). Statement 63: This we believe about the relationship between business education and students' transition to work. *Business Education Forum, 53* (1), 22–23.

Rabinowitz, S. N. (1995). Beyond testing: A vision for an ideal school-to-work assessment system. *Vocational Education Journal, 70* (3), 27–29, 52.

Roeber, E. (1996). *Emerging student assessment systems for school reform* (Report No. EDO-CG-95-11). U.S. Department of Education. (ERIC Document Reproduction Service No. ED 389 959)

Sanstead, W. G. (1993). *North Dakota curriculum frameworks, volume III* (Available from the North Dakota Department of Public Instruction, North Dakota Capitol Building, 600 E. Boulevard Avenue, Dept. 201, Floors 9, 10, and 11, Bismarck, ND 58505-0440)

Weimer, M. (Ed.). (1999). Course portfolios: The latest thinking and a new resource. *The Teaching Professor, 13* (2), 3.

Weimer, M. (Ed.). (1999). Instructional mentoring: A potpourri of activities. *The Teaching Professor, 13* (1), 4.

Weimer, M. (Ed.). (1999). Learning-centered environments. *The Teaching Professor, 13* (3), 5.

Zeliff, N., & Schultz, K. (1998). *Authentic assessment in action: Preparing for the business workplace*. Little Rock, AR: Delta Pi Epsilon.

Characteristics of Good Assessment

Judith J. Lambrecht
University of Minnesota
St. Paul, Minnesota

Educational assessment, according to the American Accounting Association (Accounting Education Change Commission, 1997) is the systematic collection, interpretation, and use of information about student characteristics, educational environment, learning outcomes, and client satisfaction to improve student performance and professional success. Sometimes assessment is considered the same as testing, but this creates a narrow image of its scope.

Testing should be viewed as only one component of the assessment process, which is systematic and interpretive. A system implies a unified and methodical approach to an activity. Interpretation involves evaluation—judging the quality of the phenomena assessed. Educational standards and criteria for levels of accomplishment can help teachers make sound judgments.

Various elements of the educational environment, not just the individual learners, can be the focus of assessment. These elements may include curriculum content and teaching practices. In any educational setting, test results are also affected by students' entry characteristics and the opportunities to learn that are presented to them. The learning outcomes of the students are not the sole outcomes of interest.

Stakeholders, including students, their parents, the business community, and the community at large—the clients—have an interest in the educational enterprise. These "clients" will have a perspective, likely each slightly different, on the overall accomplishment of program objectives.

This chapter looks more closely at the assessment activity defined above by examining the purposes, characteristics, and types of assessments. The key issue is presented of how teachers can balance the demands of large-scale assessment with the realities of classroom assessment and its integration into teaching practice.

The purposes of assessment will be described followed by the general characteristics of assessment practices, including some of the technical features that need to be present in high-quality assessment. These technical qualities will then be related to the general types of assessment devices used in business programs. Finally, the issue of balance in assessment practices will be discussed.

Purposes of Assessment

The ultimate goal of assessment is to promote high-quality instruction, since what is assessed affects instructional practices themselves and the attention that students give to their learning engagements. "Teaching to the test" and "studying for the test" are disparaging comments only when the tests or assessments do not represent worthy goals. Since schools and teachers are likely to get what they ask for, their assessment practices must capture what they expect them to capture.

The key question asked by an assessment practice is whether what was obtained is what was expected. This relationship between expected and actual outcomes is illustrated in Diagram 1 from the Accounting Education Change Commission (1997). The primary purpose of the assessment process is to detect differences between expected/desired program outcomes and actual outcomes so that program processes and outcomes can be improved.

As indicated in the diagram, the identification of clients as a group of people to satisfy suggests that assessment assists in responding to accountability expectations. Those persons or institutes that have contributed to the creation of the educational environments—such as local, state, or federal funding agencies; student and parent tuition; and other community contributors—all have expectations about learning outcomes. When expectations do not match actual outcomes, the quality of the assessment processes will assist in determining which elements of the educational environment, including curriculum content and teaching practices, together with relevant student entry characteristics, may account for the differences.

Several key concepts are important when systematic assessment is viewed as a tool for instructional improvement. While the ultimate goal of all assessment activities is program improvement, some types of assessment practices provide greater opportunity for improvement than others because they are more explicit and narrowly focused. The following discussion differentiates between two different purposes of assessment: summative and formative evaluation.

Diagram 1

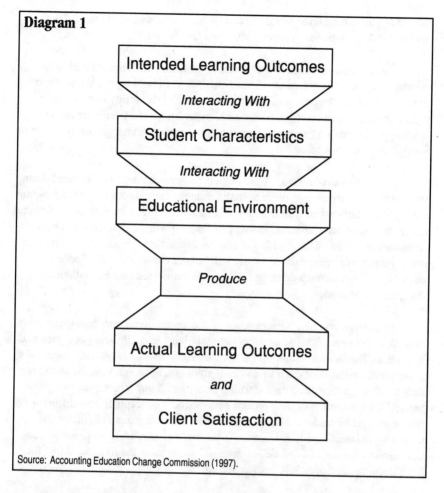

Intended Learning Outcomes

Interacting With

Student Characteristics

Interacting With

Educational Environment

Produce

Actual Learning Outcomes

and

Client Satisfaction

Source: Accounting Education Change Commission (1997).

Summative evaluation. If the purpose is to make judgments about the end result of an educational endeavor, such as a unit of instruction, a course, a program, or a class of students in a school, then the assessment is called a *summative* measure of learning outcomes. An overall evaluation is made of the success of an endeavor and the level of accomplishment attained.

If the results are positive, the program, the course, the unit of instruction, or the students themselves will be judged successful. This means the same practices may be used again with the likelihood of similar results. Or, for the students, the judgment may be that they are ready to proceed to the next level of instruction or on to other activities.

If the results are unfavorable, then the students will perhaps follow different paths, potentially remediation. The unit, the course, or the program might be changed—or other parts of the educational environment may be adapted—depending upon the quality of the assessment tools, namely, the amount of diagnostic information they provide.

The key idea to notice is that in order for the evaluations to be called summative, the assessments are carried out *after* the instructional events have been completed. The potential benefits are twofold: the ability to make judgments about the quality of the educational experiences and the nature of the learning outcomes and, given this knowledge, to propose changes for program or instructional improvement.

Formative evaluation. A different type of assessment may be used during the course of instruction in order to make changes in practices while the program is ongoing. Rather than wait until the end of a unit, course, or entire instructional program, assessments are used midway to find out whether intermediate expectations are being met. This is called *formative* evaluation because the end results of instruction are being formed, or are still "under construction." If actual outcomes at an intermediate stage do not match expected outcomes, then changes can be made.

Formative evaluation may show that the instructional materials themselves need to be changed. This means that the materials were still being designed and were, thus, the focus of attention. If the materials have already been judged of good quality because of prior assessment practices, however, then the students may need to examine their own learning activities. They might need to repeat parts of the instruction or to approach new business concepts from a different perspective. The students also might not have the background characteristics necessary to benefit from instruction as currently presented. Formative evaluation allows changes to be made "midstream" to increase the likelihood that the final learning outcomes will meet expectations.

The examples above of summative and formative evaluation include different levels of assessment based on the size of the group being examined and the breadth of the evaluative judgment to be made. Individual students may be the object of attention—are they making progress as expected (formative evaluation)? Or have they met the objectives for a given unit, course, or program (summative evaluation)? Progressing from finer levels of detail (small numbers of students, shorter instructional time periods) to larger learning experiences (larger number of students, longer time periods), individual lessons, units, or courses of instruction can be assessed to determine if they are working as expected. These judgments may be formative or summative, depending upon whether revisions can be made before students complete the learning experience.

When course and program assessments are made, the activity is likely to be summative evaluation. These are the kinds of decisions that may be possible when the outcomes of large educational components, such as courses or programs, are assessed:

- Determining whether students have passed major milestones, such as course completion, graduation, certification, or licensing;
- Selecting students for continuation into new educational settings, such as special programs, advanced courses, selective colleges, employment training programs, or employment itself;
- Determining how different schools or regions within states compare on different achievement standards, such as districtwide or statewide testing, or such as might be possible in regional, state, and national vocational student organization contests;
- Allocating resources to programs as rewards for success or to respond to remedial program needs;
- Determining program or school accreditation, such as the ability to offer special technical certification programs related to later employment opportunities; and
- Holding teachers and/or administrators accountable for their program responsibilities.

When assessments are used for summative decision-making, such as the examples above, the term "high-stakes" testing can be applied to the experiences. These assessments need to be of the highest technical quality to permit decisions to be made with confidence and integrity—as well as legality. High standards of test reliability and validity must be met. When tests are used in the classroom and teachers consider many pieces of information when making decisions about students, the psychometric standards can be a bit more relaxed (Taylor and Nolen, 1996). The characteristics of quality tests—the assessment practices themselves—are described next.

Test Characteristics

While the technical aspects of testing deserve more attention than space allows here, some key aspects of any assessment tool need to be considered before using it to make instructional decisions. Many of the traditional technical attributes of quality assessments are more difficult to obtain in what are called "nontraditional" assessment devices, such as performance assessment (Madaus and O'Dwyer, 1999) or portfolio development (Brown, 1997). These issues will be discussed when types of assessments are delineated. The following briefly describe the concepts of test validity, test reliability, and criterion- versus norm-referenced testing.

Validity. A test is valid if it measures what the authors and users intend it to measure. Implicit in this intent is an understanding of the instructional goals or outcomes and clear descriptions of the types of student performances that are likely to be exemplars of these desired capabilities. Different types of validity have been identified, such as construct validity, content validity, face validity, and criterion-related (concurrent and/or predictive) validity. Taylor and Nolen (1996) summarize the attributes of validity this way:

> *Measurement professionals generally agree that for assessments to be valid, they should (a) measure the construct they are intended to measure, (b) measure the content taught, (c) predict students' performance on subsequent assessment, and (d) provide information that is consistent with other, related sources of information. (p. 5)*

Face validity is the "appearance of reasonableness" in a test (Wiggins, 1993, p. 243). It refers not to what a test actually measures, but what it appears to measure (Anastasi, 1988). Face validity can create the kind of apparent authenticity that affects students' cooperation and motivation to engage in an assessment exercise, as well as teachers' willingness to trust the results.

Sometimes teachers are concerned about concurrent validity, meaning that two different tests intended to measure the same capability do indeed result in consistent student scores. For example, if business teachers give a theory test in a computing class about software operation and also a performance test, they could say that the tests possess concurrent validity if the rank order of students is the same on both tests. In other words, students who do well on a theory test about software use also do well on a performance test using the same software operations.

Business teachers have a special concern for predictive validity because of their interest in preparing students for employment testing. Predictive validity is the relationship between one test and a test administered later in time that is intended to measure the same competency. For example, a teacher could argue that classroom tests measuring software performance have predictive validity for later commercial software certification tests if students who do well on the classroom tests also score high on the certification exams.

Teachers need specific understandings about validity that help them think about the relationships between assessment practices and the goals and objectives of a course. Taylor and Nolen (1996) describe a classroom teacher's perspective about test validity this way:

> *Validity ... is a multidimensional construct that resides, not in the test, but in the relationship between any assessment and its context (including the instructional practices and the examinee), the construct it is to measure, and the consequences of its interpretation and use. Translated to the classroom, this means that validity encompasses (a) how assessments draw out the learning, (b) how*

*assessments fit with the educational context and instructional
strategies used, and (c) what occurs as a result of assessments,
including the full range of outcomes from feedback, grading, and
placement, to students' self-concepts and behaviors, to students'
constructions about the subject disciplines. (p. 6)*

Reliability. A frequent admonition to teachers regarding reliability is that
a test cannot be considered a valid measure if it is not first a reliable one
(Mehrens and Lehmann, 1991). A test is reliable if it measures consistently what
it is designed to measure. This means that the test is internally consistent when
each part of the test, such as each item, is measuring the same student attribute or
psychological construct.

Reliability also means that the test yields a consistent score when
administered on two different occasions, or when administered by different test
administrators. A third meaning of reliability is called "inter-rater" reliability.
When different persons score the same test, they obtain similar scores. Evidence of inter-rater reliability is particularly important for open-ended types of
tests, such as essays and performance exams. Forced-choice tests, such as
multiple-choice and true-false, are considered more objective because there is
greater likelihood that different persons scoring the exam will obtain the same
result.

Technical evidence for reliability is generally available for instruments
used in large-scale testing situations (such as program and school evaluation
programs) and for instruments used in research projects. Classroom teachers
seldom have time or the occasion to collect reliability data. Taylor and Nolen
(1996) describe the situation of classroom teachers this way when they argue for
a broader conception of what test reliability means:

*Discussion of reliability in many textbooks, however, is based on the
notion that assessment takes place at a single time and that summary decisions are made about examinees based on single testing
events. In the classroom, teachers are engaged in ongoing assessment over time and across many dimensions of behavior. Like
motivation researchers, teachers see giving students choices about
assignments as a way to increase student motivation and engagement. While individualization of instruction may result in better
achievement and motivation, it means that standardization is very
difficult. In addition, few teachers have the time or the inclination
to administer parallel test forms to see whether students' scores are
consistent; and psychometric techniques developed for looking at
internal consistency of exams are not appropriate for many forms of
classroom assessment ... Teachers do, however, collect many sources
of information about student learning—not only through tests but*

through a range of formal and informal assessments: homework, classroom work, projects, quizzes. If this information is relevant to their learning targets, teachers could make reasonable generalizations about students' learning. (pp. 9-10)

Because of the complexity of day-to-day classroom teaching, Taylor and Nolen (1996) recommend viewing test reliability along two dimensions: (1) determining the dependability of assessments made about students; and (2) determining the degree of consistency in making decisions across students and across similar types of work. Dependability comes from using a variety of high quality (valid) assessment tools, and consistency comes from using scoring criteria that are public, clear, and used consistently across students and across assessment experiences. The nature of scoring criteria is usually of two basic types—criterion-referenced and norm-referenced.

Criterion-referenced testing. A test is said to be "criterion referenced" when a student's score is evaluated against an external performance standard, not against the performance of peers. The criteria for the standards are expressed in terms of desirable characteristics for the intended learning outcome. These may be expressed as a rubric in which various levels of performance are described and assigned numerical scores.

Criterion-referenced exams have a fundamental norm reference even if the norm group is not the immediate group of student peers. The criteria established for program/course objectives have generally been developed with reference to what the typical student is able to do at a given point in an educational sequence.

The criteria may also be based on what entry-level business employees are expected to be able to do. The norm group is then the hypothetical typical, entry-level employee, not experienced workers in a field. In a job setting, the criteria for performance may change because the student has gained understandings about a particular business setting that affects the level of performance that can reasonably be expected. In other words, there is always a judgment, frequently made by a group of professionals, about what is both exemplary and what is reasonable when criteria are developed for criterion-referenced assessments.

Norm-referenced testing. When a student's performance on a test is evaluated in relation to a particular norm group, such as the class of which the student is a part, the student's work can be described in relation to the class average or other statistical measures of relative class standing. Norm-referenced testing is more common in schoolwide or state-level assessment programs with state or national student groups used for the norm reference point. Placement and entrance exams also use norm-referenced scoring with the norms obtained from previous applicants or groups of successful scholars or jobholders.

The purpose of an exam determines whether it makes sense to compare student accomplishments against a preset criterion or against designated group norms. In the classroom, if an exam has never been administered before, such as many teacher-made tests, and its difficulty is unknown, it may be reasonable to use class norms as a basis for grade assignments. This can avoid the result of awarding all "As" on an easy exam (unless the important criteria have all been met and this is reasonable), or all "Fs" on an exam that is more difficult than anticipated. Ultimately, the teacher needs to decide how well a given exam represents important course goals and what opportunities have been available to actually teach the key concepts or skills.

In the classroom, important exams or other performance opportunities are refined as they are reused. This refinement makes it possible to describe performance outcomes in a way that (1) represents high standards and important learning outcomes and (2) represents reasonable expectations for students at given levels of instructional development. As suggested by Taylor and Nolen (1996), these assessments will be of a variety of types and possibly change in response to students' interests and needs.

Types of Assessments

The possibilities for assessment instruments are described succinctly by Madaus and O'Dwyer (1999), all of which are familiar to business teachers:

> Since testing was first introduced as a policy mechanism in China in 210 B.C.E. (Before Christian Era), there have been only four ways to sample behavior from a domain. First, you can ask the person to supply an oral or written answer to a series of questions (e.g., essay questions, short-answer questions, oral disputations). Second, you can ask a person to produce a product (e.g., a portfolio of artwork, a research paper, a chair, a piece of cut glass). Third, you can require a person to perform an act to be evaluated against certain criteria (e.g., conduct a chemistry experiment, read aloud from a book, repair a carburetor, drive a car). Finally, and historically the most recent, you can have an examinee select an answer to a question or a posed problem from among several options (i.e., the multichoice or true/false item). (p. 689)

The first three types of instruments described above can be combined into what today would be called "performance assessment": the requirement that examinees construct/supply answers, produce, or perform something for evaluation.

In their critique of performance testing, Madaus and O'Dwyer (1999) identify the tension that exists between performance testing and the need for efficient ways to assess large groups of students in a society that demands account-ability and evidence of competence for the awarding of valued credentials:

We argue that changes in assessment technology over the last two centuries—from oral to written, from qualitative to quantitative, from short answer to multiple choice—were all geared toward increasing efficiency and making the assessment systems more manageable, standardized, easily administered, objective, reliable, comparable, and inexpensive, particularly as the numbers of examinees increased. (p. 689)

The essence of this argument is that performance assessment is an old, not a new, idea. Performance testing is also perhaps a more authentic form of assessment than the so-called objective assessments now being criticized for focusing on lower-levels of instructional outcomes. Forced-choice types of testing instruments have been widely criticized (Baron and Wolf, 1996; Burger, 1998; Kerka, 1995; Marzano and Pickering, 1997; Rothman, 1995; Wiggins, 1993; Zeliff and Schultz, 1998). Their weakness is that they ask mostly for the recall of facts and isolated bits of information (decontextualized declarative knowledge) rather than engaging students in the kinds of outcomes valued in places outside the school, in their communities, and later employment sites.

Business teachers have long depended upon the full spectrum of assessment types. The four major types outlined by Madaus and O'Dwyer (1999) above could further be enumerated as the following, ranging from the more explicit or "objective" to those offering more open-ended and subjective judgments:

a. *Forced-Choice*, including multiple-choice, matching, and true/false examinations.
b. *Essay Questions*, including short-answer and completion-type questions.
c. *Performance Tasks*, including computer applications, practice sets, simulations, student reports, and projects of a wide variety of types.
d. *Portfolios*, including longer-term compilations of all of the above types of items. The intent might be to show progress over time or to present exemplary products at a commencement point.
e. *Teacher Observations*, ranging from formal observations of key processes using checklists to informal, anecdotal records.
f. *Student Self-Evaluation*, applying criteria and rubrics developed by teachers or by students themselves.

Of all these, the performance exam has historically had a prominent place in the business teacher's repertoire of assessment tools. It has the essential characteristic of face validity—it asks for the kinds of outcomes that are valued in the workplace. Performance testing presents the possibility of asking students to make decisions, prioritize work, and engage in practices that have a counterpart in business settings. As such, the performance exam is the conspicuous choice for recognizing the inextricable mix of students' affective, cognitive, and psychomotor capabilities.

For education as a whole, performance tests are part of the educational reform movement (Burger, 1998; Wiggins, 1993). Performance tests are thought to be more responsive to the view of learners as constructors of knowledge in social contexts as opposed to consumers of knowledge transmitted from persons in positions of authority. Constructivist assumptions about learning ask for more exploratory or problem-based styles of learning. Such learning settings, in turn, ask for assessment practices that are responsive to the diversity of students' constructions.

As valuable as such performances are for learning, they present serious technical difficulties that make summative evaluation, particularly for high-stakes purposes, quite problematic. Outlined below is a short summary (Madaus and O'Dwyer, 1999) of the serious problems being encountered. Performance assessments that generally involve large numbers of pupils are

1. Less efficient, more difficult to administer, more disruptive to school organization, and more time-consuming than multiple-choice testing programs;
2. Not as easily standardized in terms of conditions of support for teachers within a school administering them and in terms of the actual administration itself, leading to a lack of comparability of results;
3. As vulnerable to manipulation as are multiple-choice tests in high-stakes situations;
4. Sometimes insufficiently reliable for confident use;
5. Sample a considerably smaller portion of pupil performance, raising questions about the generalizability of results to the larger domain of interest; and
6. Considerably more costly than traditional, commercially available multiple-choice tests. (p. 693)

Summary

The need for large-scale assessment, and its accompanying critique, is part of a larger social movement toward more uniform educational standards, whether these standards are locally developed, proposed by professional organizations, developed at the state level, or recommended by the national government. Much of this standards setting effort is defended as being in response to the need for economic competitiveness and the need for students to be prepared for a dynamic, information-rich, global economy (Resnick and Wirt, 1996; Stasz, 1996).

The desired learner outcomes focus heavily on processes, such as those identified by the SCANS report (Secretary's Commission on Achieving Necessary Skills, 1991) and other national skills-setting efforts (Lankard, 1995; Resnick and Wirt, 1996). Both processes and content standards are set forth in statements issued for particular subject areas, such as the *National Standards for Business Education* (National Business Education Association, 1995).

Standards setting and the consequent assessment are complex areas described well by Stake (1999) in this statement about the mix of goal statements and school assessment:

Goal statements are simplifications. The real purposes of education are far more complex than those represented in goal statements and formal assessments. Facts, theories, and reasoning exist and function not just in isolation, but interactively, innovatively, and in a range of contexts. We hold a vast inventory of expectations, partly ineffable and often only apparent in our disappointment when students fall short. That immense inventory is approximated by the informal assessment of teachers much better than by the articulated lists of goals. (p. 669)

The tension that Stake (1999) describes is the same as that identified by Taylor and Nolen (1996) in their critique of psychometric test properties and the actual practices of teachers in classrooms that need to be responsive to a wide diversity of student needs. The purpose of assessment is to improve teaching and learning. But, to do this, the difference between large-scale summative assessment needs to be kept conceptually separate from the formative purposes of assessment that allow teachers to be responsive to students' needs.

The challenge for business teachers is to balance the demands of broad system-wide, even nationally set, goals and standards with the realities of students' needs and opportunities for learning in particular classrooms. The key issue or question is how to accomplish this. The model for assessment planning adopted by the American Accounting Association (Accounting Education Change Commission, 1997) was used to introduce this chapter. It is fitting to summarize this large area of professional responsibility by presenting the Principles of Good Practice for Assessing Student Learning that the American Accounting Association has adopted. These Principles, in turn, have been adapted from those developed by the American Association for Higher Education (AAHE Assessment Forum, 1992):

- The assessment of student learning begins with educational values.
- Assessment is more effective when it reflects an understanding of learning as multidimensional, integrated, and revealed in performance over time.
- Assessment works best when the programs it seeks to improve have clear, explicitly stated purposes.
- Assessment requires attention to outcomes but also and equally to the experiences that lead to those outcomes.
- Assessment works best when it is ongoing, not episodic.
- Assessment fosters wider improvement when representatives from across the educational community are involved.

- Assessment makes a difference when it begins with issues of use and illuminates questions that people really care about.
- Assessment is most likely to lead to improvement when it is part of a larger set of conditions that promote change.
- Through assessment, educators meet responsibilities to students and to the public. (pp. 2-3)

Assessment is not an adjunct to teaching. It is the essence of teaching in that it provides essential feedback to both teachers and learners about the results of their efforts. The challenge is to make worthy use of students' time as they engage in efforts that will affect their future capabilities and life endeavors. Stakeholders of several types have an interest in these outcomes—hence the prominence today of standards setting from the national level down to the local school district.

Business teachers, along with all teachers, need to participate in choosing goals that are worthy of their attention and articulating these goals in meaningful ways as they develop instructional engagements. Whatever the source of external standards setting and criteria development, it is the individual teacher's selection and/or development of specific assessment practices that matters most. Through teachers' understanding, use, and contextually sensitive interpretation of a variety of high-quality assessment practices, the ultimate goal of assessment can be realized—the improvement of instruction.

References

Accounting Education Change Commission. (1997). *Assessment for the new curriculum: A guide for professional accounting programs* [Online]. Available: http://206.170.119.32/pubs/assessment/index.htm

American Association for Higher Education (AAHE) Assessment Forum. (1992, December). *Assessment principles of good practice.* Washington, DC: AAHE.

Anastasi, A. (1988). *Psychological testing* (6th ed.). New York: Macmillan.

Baron, J. B., & Wolf, D. P. (Eds.). (1996). Performance-based student assessment: Challenges and possibilities. In *Ninety-fifth yearbook of the national society for the study of education, part I.* Chicago: University of Chicago Press.

Brown, B. L. (1997). Portfolio assessment: Missing link in student evaluation. In *Trends and issues alerts.* Columbus, OH: ERIC Clearinghouse on Adult, Career, and Vocational Education.

Burger, D. (1998). Designing a sustainable standards-based assessment system. Aurora, CO: Mid-continent Regional Educational Laboratory (McREL) [Online]. Available: http://www.mcrel.org/resources/noteworthy/assessment-system-printer.asp

Kerka, S. (1995). *Techniques for authentic assessment.* Columbus, OH: ERIC Clearinghouse on Adult, Career, and Vocational Education.

Lankard, B. A. (1995). Business/industry standards and vocational program accountability. Columbus, OH: ERIC Clearinghouse on Adult, Career, and Vocational Education. (ERIC Digest No. 157)

Madaus, G. F., & O'Dwyer, L. M. (1999, May). A short history of performance assessment: Lessons learned. *Phi Delta Kappan, 80* (9), 688–695.

Madaus, G., Raczek, A. E., & Hoffmann, T. (1997). What is a test? The Center for the Study of Testing, Evaluation, and Educational Policy [Online]. Available: http://www.csteep.bc.edu/ctest

Marzano, R. J., & Pickering, D. J. (1997). *Dimensions of learning: Teacher's manual* (2nd ed.). Aurora, CO: Mid-continent Regional Educational Laboratory (McREL).

Mehrens, W. A., & Lehmann, I. J. (1991). *Measurement and evaluation in education and psychology* (4th ed.). Fort Worth, TX: Holt, Rinehart, and Winston, Inc.

National Business Education Association. (1995). *National standards for business education: What America's students should know and be able to do in business.* Reston, VA: National Business Education Association.

Resnick, L. B., & Wirt, J. G. (Eds.). (1996). *Linking school and work: Roles for standards and assessment.* San Francisco: Jossey-Bass Inc., Publishers.

Rothman, R. (1995). *Measuring up: Standards, assessment, and school reform.* San Francisco: Jossey-Bass Inc., Publishers.

Secretary's Commission on Achieving Necessary Skills (SCANS). (1991). *What work requires of schools: A SCANS report for America 2000.* Washington, DC: U.S. Department of Labor.

Stake, R. (1999, May). The goods on American education. *Phi Delta Kappan, 80* (9), 668–72.

Stasz, C. (1996, November). *The economic imperative behind school reform: A review of the literature.* (MDS-1028). Berkeley, CA: National Center for Research in Vocational Education, University of California at Berkeley.

Taylor, C. S., & Nolen, S. B. (1996). What does the psychometrician's classroom look like?: Reframing assessment concepts in the context of learning. *Education Policy Analysis Archives* [Online], *4* (17), 1–35. Available: http://olam.ed.asu.edu/apaa/v4n17.html

Wiggins, G. P. (1993). *Assessing student performance: Exploring the purpose and limits of testing.* San Francisco: Jossey-Bass Inc., Publishers.

Zeliff, N., & Schultz, K. (1998). *Authentic assessment in action: Preparing for the business workplace.* Little Rock, AR: Delta Pi Epsilon.

The Evolution of Assessment, Testing, and Evaluation

George A. Mundrake
Ball State University
Muncie, Indiana

Throughout the history of business education, concern for assessment, testing, and evaluation has driven the educational process. Both student and teacher performance have been ever-present factors in determining if the goals of business education have been met. Terminology that describes methods of measuring the outcomes of the educational process has varied depending on the contemporary social, educational, and economic environments.

Definitions and/or interpretations of these methods are important because the politics of funding, program priorities, and distribution of classroom resources are contingent on the ways programs and students are evaluated. In addition to local and state concerns over student achievement, national standards and federal funding issues require the interpretation of the student and teacher educational outcomes.

The definitions of assessment, testing, and evaluation are as varied as those who use them and the times in which they are made. Historically, these definitions depend on the interpreter's stake in the educational process. Political leaders and taxpayers may view them as a measure of "return on investment." Teachers and students may view them as indicators of their accomplishments or as a form of performance appraisal for their work; and parents and students may view them as measures of accomplishment and potential for future performance (or lack of accomplishment, depending upon the results).

Assessment, testing, and evaluation are terms that have been used to point fingers at the failures, as well as the successes, of the educational system. But what exactly do these terms mean? Can we even agree on their definitions? Clarification may be accomplished by looking at their historical evolution.

Historical Considerations

In the mid-1840s, evaluation involved the oral questioning of students and interpretation of their answers by teachers. By the turn of the century, the "scientific measurement movement" became popular, and standardized written tests began to appear. Since the 1940s, student evaluation has been synonymous with the written test. The written test was the primary form of evaluation in the 1940s and still is an often-used tool.

Because of increasing rates of change in technology and the workplace over the past two decades, views and concepts of assessment, testing, and evaluation have become less clear. The yardsticks used to measure the performances have not always been accurate. During the 1980s, emphasis was placed on teacher, school, and student performance. Results from state programs such as career ladder programs for teachers, the *A Nation at Risk* report (U.S. National Commission on Excellence in Education, 1983), and the Secretary's Commission on Achieving Necessary Skills (SCANS) national report (U.S. Department of Labor, 1991) painted a somewhat grim picture of our educational system.

Being able to show concrete, numeric, or empirical evidence of results of educational processes and programs (usually in the form of test scores) became a nationwide priority. Such programs reflected the "get tough" attitude of the time.

Today, state departments of education and national organizations are designing standards that promote educational accountability by utilizing more reasonable and varied methods of assessment including rubrics (sets of scoring criteria), portfolios, expected outcomes or performance expectations, and other nonobjective forms of evaluation.

What Is Assessment?

The interpretation of the word assessment has changed most significantly over the years. Traditionally, assessment has been associated with a proactive and preinstructional review of student needs. This review or "needs assessment" was an effort to find out what should be taught. Business educators used advisory boards, graduate follow-up surveys, and research in the business community to identify trends and determine what to teach.

Today, assessment has a much broader definition that more closely resembles the traditional view of evaluation. The view of assessment has evolved into a more formative approach that addresses the question, "How am I doing?" Assessment is an ongoing process involving the systematic collection, analysis, and integration of information (Hoy and Gregg, 1994). This information may include formal assessments (tests and other written items) and informal samples of work by students (portfolios, essays, presentations, rubrics, performance check sheets, and other activity appraisal formats). This broader interpretation takes into consideration the differences in learning styles of students.

Still another view of assessment addresses problems with written tests. "Authentic assessment" (Darling-Hammond, Ancess, and Falk, 1995) calls for formative alternatives to written tests in the form of assessments that mimic real-life tasks. In order to be "authentic," the assessments must be representative of performance in the field, must evaluate "essentials" of performance against well-articulated standards, and often must allow students to present their work orally and publicly.

A more pragmatic approach to assessment as a systematic collection, review, and use of information about educational programs undertaken for the purpose of improving student learning and development includes assessment of programs, instruction, student performance, and workplace performance (Palomba and Banta, 1999). This wider view includes program assessments, performance evaluations, written tests, or any other form of evaluation as assessment.

What Is Testing?

Perhaps the most widely used and least understood form of measurement is the test. Tests may be in written, oral, or performance-based formats. Properly constructed tests can be highly reliable and valid measurements of student performance; however, they are difficult to construct and even more difficult to maintain and interpret.

The use of written tests as a "scientific measurement" of performance has been challenged. Critics of the use of written tests cite the following limitations:

- Inability to evaluate high-order tasks or problem solving (Davidson, Webster, and Truell, 1999);
- Lack of reflection on current understandings of how students learn;
- Overuse, leading to a narrow curriculum; and
- Inability to be used for diagnostic applications.

Though many of these criticisms may be valid, part of the problem may be a lack of knowledge and training on the part of a classroom teacher about proper test construction, usage, and interpretation of results. Courses on assessment, test construction, and evaluation have been dropped from many teacher education programs.

What Is Evaluation?

In the classroom environment, the term, evaluation, has evolved to encompass a more summative meaning as an overall measure of student performance. This includes a mix of samplings that are used to determine a summative grade for student performance. These samples of performance include tests, projects, learning activities, and other assignments.

Evaluation involves judgmental weighting of these components and the application of a grade. In a broader sense, it involves evaluation of the program or curriculum, the teachers, and the school in general.

Instructional Models and Assessment, Testing, and Evaluation

For years educators have used instructional models in some form or another to develop curriculum and educational programs as well as to create courses. The models usually involve these steps:

- Needs assessment,
- Development of objectives,
- Selection of evaluation methods,
- Instructional delivery plans,
- Instruction, and
- Some form of evaluation of the results of instruction.

Early models assumed an ending point for courses and a particular curriculum. These models tended to use a more static approach and worked well when there were not too many changes in the curriculum or the world in general. Figure 1 is a stepwise or static model.

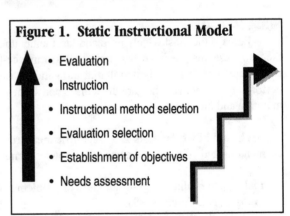

Figure 1. Static Instructional Model

- Evaluation
- Instruction
- Instructional method selection
- Evaluation selection
- Establishment of objectives
- Needs assessment

Business educators have traditionally been faced with change; however, before 1980 they experienced changes in much longer cycles. For example, calculators were relatively similar from the 1930s into the late 1970s.

Today, much instruction about computers may be obsolete in the workplace when the student graduates. Because of the dynamic nature of the workplace, the models for development of instruction must also be dynamic. Content and concepts to be taught about computer applications must be transferable as hardware and software evolve.

Models also include more dynamic components that emphasize and recognize change and the continuing evolution of programs or courses. Schrag and

Poland (1988) suggested a system for teaching business education that included these dynamic components. Feedback along the way in the form of assessments of each step is incorporated into the model. Today's models stress the view of education as a lifelong, ongoing process. Formative measures ("How am I doing?") are stressed more than summative results ("How did I do?"). Figure 2 is a dynamic model.

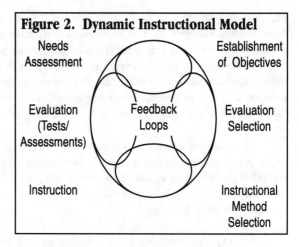

Figure 2. Dynamic Instructional Model

Objectives and Taxonomies: Necessities for Assessment, Testing, and Evaluation

In order to evaluate any performance or progress, one must have a goal to reach, an objective to satisfy, or criteria for comparison. The degrees to which these objectives are met are determined by learning domains (cognitive, affective, psychomotor) and taxonomies or levels of learning. In some cases, educators are still using objective strategies that were developed during the 1930s but that are still effective and appropriate. In some form or another, these strategies include the following steps:

- Establishment of general objectives,
- Classification of the objectives into degrees of expected outcomes (taxonomies),
- Clarification of the objectives in terms that can be measured (behavioral objectives),
- Examination of situations and indicators that will show if the objective has been met,
- Selection of measurement techniques,
- Collection of performance data, and
- Comparison of performance to objectives.

Models of course and curriculum development emphasize the importance of objectives at all levels (school, curriculum, program, and classroom).

Reliability and Validity: Intrinsic Problems of Assessment, Testing, and Evaluation

The primary concern of testing, evaluation, and/or assessment should be the interpretation of the results. The interpretation may be summative to prove results of instruction or to answer the question, "How did the student do?" This interpretation may provide a comparison of performance with other students using a norm-referenced standard (based on statistical analysis of tests taken by many students) or by using criterion-referenced tests (how well objectives are met). Other interpretations view education as an ongoing, dynamic, lifelong process, with a more formative interpretation that addresses the questions of "How are the students doing?" or "Is there improvement?"

Since all evaluation involves some form of judgment or interpretation, two major concerns about testing and methods of assessment are inherent: validity and reliability of the measuring instrument. No matter what form the measurement instrument takes, both of these factors are essential for evaluating performance or progress correctly.

Validity is the most important criterion for an evaluative tool. An assessment must truly measure what it purports to measure. The basic types of validity include:

- Content validity—How well does the test measure the content of the course or curriculum?
- Construct validity—Does the test relate to a set of complex attitudes, mental skills, or appreciations?
- Concurrent validity—How does the test compare with a previously established test, knowledge, or performance?
- Predictive validity—How does the test predict or compare with future knowledge or performance?

Reliability is a measure of the ability of an instrument to measure consistently and without error. Assessments can be reliable but not valid. Longstanding, traditional views of evaluation insist that a test or assessment tool cannot be valid if it is not reliable. Validity, when proved, also proves reliability.

In a teaching environment, the major emphasis is on the content validity of measuring devices or assessments. Does the assessment measure what it should measure? Giving students a test that covers the life of Shakespeare in an introductory computer class, for example, would not be considered valid for the subject matter.

More recent views of validity (Messick, 1995) also include substantive validity (emphasis on theoretical rationale), generalizability validity (generalization to the population across populations), external validity (applications to multitrait and multimethod comparison), and consequential validity (bias, fairness, justice, and social consequences of assessment to society). These more recent views of validity illustrate a trend favoring assessments other than traditional written tests.

Reliability involves the consistency of a measurement's ability to measure. For example, a siding sales scam artist could "short stick" a customer by using a yardstick that was less than a yard to estimate the amount of siding that would be needed on a house. Using the short stick to measure the amount of siding needed would consistently yield an inaccurate result, even if measured numerous times. The measuring device in this case would measure the same over and over and could be considered "reliable" even though it is highly inaccurate. A test with vague, confusing, and misleading questions, and questions unrelated to the course content, might yield consistent results if given to groups of students, even though it does not measure the true content of the course.

In testing, reliability traditionally has been measured by using statistical analysis. This analysis is performed by statistically comparing scores on even- and odd-numbered questions or by scoring the first and second halves of the test separately (split halves). The scores are then correlated, yielding a number between -1 and +1, or a correlation coefficient. The closer the correlation is to +1, the more "internally consistent" the test. "Standardized" tests usually must have a correlation of at least +.80 to be deemed "reliable."

One of the basic criticisms of many assessment tools is the lack of reliability of the instruments. Correlation of scores to establish reliability on portfolios, presentations, and other assessments is statistically a difficult task. Evaluation and scoring of these assessments are highly subjective. Some educators dismiss this lack of "statistical reliability" with the theory that there can be validity without reliability (Moss, 1994). This view suggests that inconsistency of student performance does not invalidate assessment and suggests the need to search for a more comprehensive interpretation of the results.

On a more pragmatic note, most teachers are not the only evaluators. Evaluation of educational products and programs comes from parents, the community, government, funding agencies, and numerous other sources. Evaluation does not end with the classroom teacher.

Summary

Assessment, testing, and evaluation are terms used to describe ways to measure the outcomes of the educational process. Assessment is the term currently used to describe all aspects of evaluation and testing. New forms of assessment, including portfolio assessment, negotiated assessment, performance assessment, authentic assessment, and responsive evaluation, have entered the lexicon of education. At the same time, criticism of written tests increases and the call for accountability grows louder.

Some newer forms of assessment have an inherent lack of statistical reliability. If educators choose these new forms, they must find better ways to prove and improve their reliability. The use of content matrices, expected outcome lists, performance expectation lists, and other rubric-based evaluation forms may help increase the reliability and validity of these instruments.

Teachers and future teachers need to learn more about assessment, testing, and evaluation through formal and ongoing study of the field of educational assessment and its tools. Teacher education programs should include more emphasis on evaluation and assessment to help teachers make wiser choices about assessment methods. Too often tests are selected from supplemental materials in sources that are not reliable, are not valid, and are constructed improperly.

For students, grades are their academic payroll (Mundrake, 1988). No one wants a paycheck that is inaccurate. Students deserve assessment tools that can give valid and reliable measures of their progress. For teachers, evaluation implies a measure of their performance in the classroom. They, too, deserve to have the best measures of their work. In a broader sense, assessments measure courses, curriculum, and schools in general. The sometimes frustrating, often confusing, and usually controversial issues about assessment, testing, and evaluation must be addressed to advance the quality of education.

References

Darling-Hammond, L., Ancess, J., & Falk, B. (1995). *Authentic assessment in action*. New York: Teacher College Press, Columbia University.

Davidson, C., Webster, L., & Truell, A. D. (1999). Problem-based exams versus objective exams as a predictor of final student achievement. *Delta Pi Epsilon Journal, 40,* 26–35.

Hardaway, M. (1966). *Testing and evaluation in business education*. Cincinnati, OH: South-Western Publishing Company.

Hoy, C., & Gregg, N. (1994). *Assessment: The special educator's role*. Pacific Grove, CA: Brooks/Cole Publishing Company.

Messick, S. (1995). Validity of psychological assessment: Validation of inferences from person's responses and performance as scientific inquiry into scoring meaning. *American Psychologist, 9,* 741–749.

Moss, P. A. (1994). Can there be validity without reliability? *Educational Researcher, 23,* 5–12.

Mundrake, G. A. (1988, May). The academic payroll. *Business Education Forum, 42* (8), 3–4.

Palomba, C. A., & Banta, T. W. (1999). *Assessment essentials: Planning, implementing, and improving assessment in higher education*. San Francisco: Jossey-Bass Inc., Publishers.

Schrag, A. F., & Poland, R. P. (1988). *A system for teaching business education*. New York: McGraw-Hill Book Company.

Secretary's Commission on Achieving Necessary Skills (SCANS). (1991). *What work requires of schools: A SCANS report for America 2000*. Washington, DC: U.S. Department of Labor.

U.S. National Commission on Excellence in Education. (1983). *A Nation at risk: The imperative for educational reform.* Washington, DC: U.S. Department of Education.

Developing Appropriate Assessment for a Business Teacher Education Program

Linda Cresap and Julianne Eklund
Minot State University
Minot, North Dakota

Assessment, by documenting competence and providing continuous feedback, can help ensure that future business educators are well qualified to teach students the skills needed for success in the 21st century workplace. Designing and implementing an assessment plan for a business education program can be accomplished efficiently and effectively in three developmental stages: initial planning, technique selection, and ongoing evaluation. This chapter provides an example of how these three stages were followed in developing an assessment plan for the business teacher education program at Minot State University (MSU) in Minot, North Dakota. A review of the literature is followed by a discussion of the MSU plan.

Related Literature

Initial planning. Establishing an effective assessment plan begins with identifying the role of faculty in the development process. Doherty and Patton (1994) suggest that faculty be given responsibility for the plan's design and implementation. This strategy encourages their acceptance of assessment by giving them the opportunity to understand and develop the plan. Faculty are integral to improving student learning; thus, if improvement of student learning is the ultimate goal of assessment, they need to be actively involved and take ownership in the assessment plan development (Doherty and Patton, 1994).

Applebaum (1994) suggests a senior faculty member take the lead in the project. In business teacher education, this strategy is especially useful; business education's everchanging nature deems it necessary for an assessment leader to have extensive knowledge of the curriculum, students, department, and institution in order to reflect on workable design and implementation strategies.

The leader should be someone other than the department chairperson to allow the chairperson to participate as a faculty member and to alleviate any possible concerns about formal faculty evaluation becoming a part of the assessment process.

Initial assessment planning also includes developing the assessment plan framework (Roeber, 1996). This framework is established by considering institution and department mission statements and reviewing current research on competencies needed for business teachers. Next, faculty can determine program-learning goals along with specific, measurable learning objectives for each goal (Gardner, 1994). Establishing this type of assessment framework is strongly encouraged by accrediting agencies (Walvoord and Anderson, 1998).

Technique selection. Faculty should consider selecting multiple assessment techniques for assessing student learning within a program (Conrad and Wilson, 1994; Doherty and Patton, 1994; PCBEE, 1998; Prus and Johnson, 1994; Walvoord and Anderson, 1998). Assessment techniques exist for three different stages within the learning cycle: diagnostic, formative, and summative (PCBEE, 1998).

Diagnostic techniques are those applied at students' entrance to a program and most commonly take the form of standardized tests. Formative techniques focus on students demonstrating their abilities to solve problems rather than simply providing a solution. Techniques include portfolios, theses and projects, oral or comprehensive exams, and use of external examiners to review student work. Summative techniques focus on milestones achieved by students at the completion of a program and commonly rely on standardized tests as tools (PCBEE, 1998).

Walvoord and Anderson (1998), referencing the American Association of Higher Education's "Principles of Good Practice for Assessing Student Learning," suggest that the most effective assessment techniques are those that reflect an understanding of learning as multidimensional, integrated, and revealed in performance over time. This statement defines formative assessment and is exemplified in the portfolio assessment technique. Portfolios are continual, authentic, sensitive to local goals and interests, highly interactive between faculty and students, and allow for immediate feedback (Fong, 1994).

Portfolios provide the opportunity for students to demonstrate their skills in interpretation, reflection, and problem solving. Faculty can work with the students to determine appropriate contents that depict the students' learning growth leading to the outcomes desired. Student portfolios are useful in business teacher education because they create opportunities for multiple components and concepts to be measured (Fong, 1994).

When faculty review and grade students' portfolios, both students and faculty have an opportunity to exchange ideas, discuss curriculum goals, review grading criteria, and provide program feedback (Prus and Johnson, 1994). Faculty and the department benefit from this opportunity for focused discussion that can lead to program improvement.

A related technique is to create course portfolios for assessment purposes. A course portfolio captures scholarship in teaching the course and provides specific focus for course examination and discussion of teaching in a coherent way (Cerbin, 1994). The individual course can serve as an ideal context for reviewing the interplay between teaching and learning using the portfolio as a data-gathering instrument. Contents of the course portfolio vary and depend greatly on the extent of information desired and the faculty member creating the portfolio. Typical contents might include

1. A teaching statement conveying the instructor's assumptions about teaching and learning and explaining the intended learning outcomes of the course, the teaching practices to address these outcomes, and the rationale that connects the course goals to the teacher's methods;
2. An analysis of student learning based on student performance on two or more key assignments or activities representing typical teaching and learning taking place;
3. An analysis of student feedback about how teaching affects their learning in the class; and
4. A course summary describing the strengths and weaknesses of the course in terms of students' learning, analysis of these outcomes, and identification of changes that may enhance student learning in the future (Cerbin, 1994).

Completion of the faculty portfolio for a course can lead a department into an open discussion of curriculum. This assessment technique is typically in the form of a departmental review of course syllabi where faculty teaching different sections of the same course analyze the course goals and objectives, contents, and methods; they then determine a common syllabus for the course.

For business teacher educators, a syllabi review within the department may be just the technique to tie together assessment data while upgrading curriculum. Applebaum refers to this technique as an "audit" whereby faculty conduct an intensive review of course syllabi, required exercises, and samples of student projects at different stages to determine or verify goal achievement (Ewell, 1994).

Students' perceptions of their own growth can also serve as a viable assessment technique. Their perceptions can be viewed through a survey, a summative assessment technique. Student surveys, according to Gardner

(1994), yield perceptions that may lead to changes benefiting the relationship between groups. Surveys convey a sense of importance regarding the opinion of those surveyed and are a solution to covering a broad range of information in a brief manner. Exit surveys and graduate surveys are popular formats to consider.

Ongoing evaluation. "Assessment works best when it is ongoing, not episodic" (Walvoord and Anderson, 1998, p. 190). Assessment plans need to be reviewed, discussed, and revised continually to maintain their relevance to the business education curriculum. An evaluation of the assessment plan will verify whether its framework is sound and in conjunction with the institution's and department's missions. It will also reveal if the data gathered are being used for the intended purposes, and if the improvement of the business teacher education program and the enhancement of student learning are being achieved (Doherty and Patton, 1994).

One strategy for evaluating the assessment plan is to view the validity of the techniques selected. According to Prus and Johnson (1994), validity includes relevance, accuracy, and utility of the plan. A technique that is relevant measures educational objectives as directly as possible. A technique that is accurate measures educational objectives as precisely as possible. Finally, a technique that has utility provides both formative and summative results with clear implications for the improvement of the educational program. Good techniques should produce assessment results that are useful for enhancing the program, while poor techniques will be detrimental to the assessment process.

While Prus and Johnson (1994) advocate conducting a pilot test of the assessment plan, a logical strategy for business teacher educators is that with each application of the plan another pilot test takes place. Business teacher education is a rapidly changing field with curriculum that is revised continually to address the needs of graduates in the profession. Each time assessment tools are implemented and data are analyzed, faculty work to enhance curriculum based on the outcomes of the analysis and, therefore, may adjust the assessment plan on an ongoing basis.

An Example of an Assessment Plan

The Business Information Technology Department in the College of Business at Minot State University houses the business teacher education program. The department applied the three-step process in developing the business teacher education assessment plan, and a summary of this plan follows.

Initial planning. The department planning process began with the appointment of two senior faculty members to lead the project. The department chairperson was not one of these leaders. Next, the department reviewed MSU's mission statement. They also reviewed the mission statement of the university's education department since the business teacher education program is not housed in that department but is affiliated with it. A departmental statement was developed, accompanied by six broad outcome goals reflecting what faculty believe business teacher education graduates should know. Faculty created performance objectives for each goal statement. The department mission statement, program goals, and learning objectives are listed in Appendix A.

Next, faculty reviewed current courses with the goals and objectives in mind, and determined where objectives were already being addressed or should be incorporated. A new common syllabus was designed to provide students the department mission statement and goals as well as the course objectives that matched these goals. Minimum contents and reference materials were also listed on the syllabi. Individual faculty are free to develop the course methodology and assignments with the common objectives and contents in mind.

Technique selection. Faculty elected to follow a combined formative and summative strategy for assessment techniques. Three techniques are now in use for the business education program: course portfolios, syllabi review, and follow-up surveys.

The course portfolio technique requires that faculty identify samples of students' assignments that illustrate their exposure to and/or attainment of the specific assessment objectives identified for the course. Assignments selected by the course instructor might include descriptions of in-class activities, handouts used that detail assignments, samples of student work, or videotapes of student presentations. When actual student work is used, students' names are removed, and they are asked to sign a release form if they agree to allow their work to be included as an example.

The faculty also prepare a survey for students to evaluate learning objectives for each specific course. Students are asked to anonymously identify to what extent they believe each assessment objective was covered and personally attained in the course. They are also encouraged to identify activities and/or assignments where these objectives were addressed. The completed evaluations are included in the portfolio.

At the end of the semester, the department assessment committee reviews all portfolios. After this review, the committee meets with a faculty member if there is a question regarding any items in the portfolio. The form completed by the course instructor and used to evaluate the portfolio by the department assessment committee is illustrated in Appendix B.

Faculty have remained positive about the course portfolio as an assessment technique because of the multiple uses for the information gathered. In addition to looking at student learning, faculty are able to conduct a self-assessment of teaching strategies and review course materials and contents. Additionally, the portfolio becomes a tool to use in the syllabi review process, an assessment technique that focuses on curriculum revision.

The syllabi review takes place each year and is based partly on the results and reflections from the course portfolios. Faculty who teach the same course review the common components of the course and discuss objectives, content, current research and practice, and outcomes of the course portfolios. Both faculty and future students benefit from these lively discussions where course modifications are made and agreed upon. This process also provides a link for the department to review the overall assessment plan since review of objectives often leads to discussion and validation of goals and the mission statement.

The third assessment technique used in the department is a follow-up survey of business teacher education graduates. This summative technique is in the form of an exit survey completed when students register for graduation. Students are asked to identify to what degree they believe they have attained overall goals and related objectives for the program. A sample of this exit survey is located in Appendix C.

A less formal follow-up survey is also conducted by telephone (or perhaps in the future through e-mail) one year after each student graduates. This survey gathers the students' opinions of the same goals and objectives in terms of the students' actual application of and competence in the skills after one year on the job.

Ongoing evaluation. As a strategy for evaluating the assessment plan, the department meets twice yearly to discuss it. Both formative and summative data are reviewed and evaluated for relevance and accuracy. A report that reviews changes in the assessment plan is submitted each spring to the MSU campus assessment committee and the dean of institutional planning. The report provides details on assessment data collected and analyzed and summarizes outcomes and results of the assessment process.

The department views the assessment plan as a living document, continually upgraded to reflect the everchanging curriculum in business teacher education, as well as new methodology and refined techniques. The assessment process has created a cohesive program for faculty and students in the business teacher education program that is possible because of the strategies applied. The department plans instruction and content through syllabi review, analyzes coverage and methodology through course portfolios, and verifies students' perspectives of learning with the course learning survey and follow-up surveys.

Summary

Business teacher education departments might consider using the MSU business teacher education assessment plan as a model. Advantages of this plan are that it can be efficiently developed and administered and that it includes a process for incorporating assessment results as a means for quickly improving instruction. To model this assessment program, the following steps should be taken:

1. Take time to plan assessment.
   - Identify a senior faculty member, other than the department chairperson, to lead the effort.
   - Review the institution and department mission statements, as well as current research, in order to establish program learning goals and objectives.
   - Review current courses with goals and objectives in mind. Create common syllabi for each course and include the objectives.

2. Select assessment techniques.
   - Implement the course portfolio by setting up file folders for each faculty member. Each faculty member's folder should contain an evaluation sheet (Appendix B) for each course. Faculty should be instructed to complete their portion of the evaluation form throughout the semester. Also included in the portfolio should be the surveys for students to evaluate the learning objectives for each specific course. These surveys may be completed by students at the end of the semester, summarized, and included in the portfolio. At the end of the term, the portfolio should be given to the department's assessment leader for review.
   - After a review of the portfolios, gather faculty for a review session on course syllabi. Ideally, this session is held in a retreat environment, away from campus and for an extended period of time. Revise master syllabi to reflect changes noted through portfolio analysis and discussion.
   - Request that students complete the follow-up survey as they register for graduation. Provide specific instructions for completing and returning the survey. Surveys should be analyzed by the department assessment committee and results should be reported to the department.

3. Determine a schedule for ongoing evaluation of the assessment plan.
   - Meet at least once, preferably twice, yearly to discuss assessment. Discussions might include presentation of the previous semester's results, individual faculty members' reviews of changes made in courses as a result of assessment findings, and new techniques that could be pilot tested.
   - If required, complete a report for the campus summarizing the outcomes and status of the assessment plan for the time frame specified.

The business teacher education department faculty at MSU are convinced that this assessment model provides important information for improving instruction. Through assessment, faculty discuss, review, and reflect on course content on a regular basis thereby creating a contemporary, research-enhanced curriculum for their future teachers.

References

Applebaum, M. I. (1994). Assessment through the major. In J. S. Stark & A. Thomas (Eds.), Asse*ssment and program evaluation, ASHE reader series* (pp. 275–288). New York: Simon and Schuster.

Cerbin, W. (1994). The course portfolio as a tool for continuous improvement in teaching and learning. *Electronic journal on excellence in college teaching* [Online]. Available: http://ject.lib.muohio.edu/html/v5n1/v5n1-Cerbin.html

Conrad, C. F., & Wilson, R. F. (1994). Academic program reviews: Institutional approaches, expectations, and controversies. In J. S. Stark & A. Thomas (Eds.), *Assessment and program evaluation, ASHE reader series* (pp. 183–198). New York: Simon and Schuster.

Doherty, A., & Patton, G. W. (1994). Criterion three and the assessment of student academic achievement. In J. S. Stark & A. Thomas (Eds.), *Assessment and program evaluation, ASHE reader series* (pp. 763–767). New York: Simon and Schuster.

Ewell, P. T. (1994). To capture the ineffable: New forms of assessment in higher education. In J. S. Stark & A. Thomas (Eds.), *Assessment and program evaluation, ASHE reader series* (pp. 363–376). New York: Simon and Schuster.

Fong, B. (1994). Assessing the department major. In J. S. Stark & A. Thomas (Eds.), *Assessment and program evaluation, ASHE reader series* (pp. 413–421). New York: Simon and Schuster.

Gardner, D. E. (1994). Five evaluation frameworks: Implications for decision making in higher education. In J. S. Stark & A. Thomas (Eds.), *Assessment and program evaluation, ASHE reader series* (pp. 7–19). New York: Simon and Schuster.

Policies Commission for Business and Economic Education (PCBEE). (1998). *Policy statement 59: This we believe about assessing student achievement in business education* [Online]. Available: http://www.nbea.org/curfpolicy.html

Prus, J., & Johnson, R. (1994). A critical review of student assessment options. In J. S. Stark & A. Thomas (Eds.), *Assessment and program evaluation, ASHE reader series* (pp. 603–618). New York: Simon and Schuster.

Roeber, E. D. (1996). Guidelines for the development and management of performance assessments. *Practical Assessment Research & Evaluation* [Online]. Available: http://ericae.net/pare/getvn.asp?v=5&n=7

Walvoord, B. E., & Anderson, V. J. (1998). *Effective grading: A tool for learning and assessment.* San Francisco: Jossey-Bass Inc., Publishers.

Appendix A

Mission Statement

The primary mission of the Department of Business Information Technology's business teacher education program is to engage students in learning opportunities focused on developing technical competency, global perspective, communication skills, and professional and human relationship skills. Course work emphasizes situational analysis, critical thinking, creativity, and application as such skills are used in a reflective decision-making process. Courses are built around the ARK model, whereby students practice decision making through Action, Reflection, and Knowledge.

Program Goals

1. Students identify and demonstrate their levels of computer, information, and technological literacy.
2. Students demonstrate knowledge of communication skills.
3. Students demonstrate professional attitudes and conduct.
4. Students demonstrate global awareness.
5. Students demonstrate an ability to reflect and to apply critical-thinking skills when solving problems.
6. Students demonstrate and experience real-life applications in a nonacademic environment.

Learning Objectives

Program Goal I. Students identify and demonstrate their levels of computer, information, and technological literacy.

1. Students demonstrate knowledge of basic components of a computer system.
2. Students demonstrate knowledge of computer operating systems.
3. Students demonstrate knowledge of software application tools.
4. Students demonstrate ability to locate, create, analyze, interpret, manage, and use data.
5. Students demonstrate knowledge of technology.

Program Goal II. Students demonstrate knowledge of communication skills.

6. Students organize a written and an oral message coherently and effectively.
7. Students use technology for communication.
8. Students demonstrate ability to research a topic, prepare a report, and present their findings to all organizational levels.
9. Students demonstrate the ability to work in teams.

Program Goal III. Students demonstrate professional attitudes and conduct.

10. Students practice ethical conduct in their decision making and behavior.

11. Students practice professional appearance.
12. Students demonstrate acceptable social business behavior.

Program Goal IV. *Students demonstrate global awareness.*

13. Students demonstrate the ability to apply concepts in a global setting.
14. Students demonstrate their understanding of cultural differences.

Program Goal V. *Students demonstrate an ability to reflect and to apply critical-thinking skills when solving problems.*

15. Students demonstrate use of critical-thinking skills when solving problems.
16. Students demonstrate the ability to transfer a concept to a specific situation.
17. Students demonstrate ability to interpret and synthesize information.

Program Goal VI. *Students demonstrate and experience real-life applications in a nonacademic environment.*

18. Students observe technological applications in real-life settings.
19. Students apply skills in projects, practicums, internships, and/or student teaching.

Appendix B

Department of Business Information Technology Portfolio Checklist

Course Name
_____

Course Number
_____

Instructor
_____

Semester: ☐ F   ☐ SP   ☐ SM

Objective(s) Being Addressed:

_____

_____

_____

Description of Assignment and Sample (if applicable):

_____

_____

_____

_____

_____

Enclosures:

☐ Assignment   ☐ Video student work sample

☐ Written student work sample   ☐ Other, please describe:

                                          _____

* * * * *

Assessment Committee Review Date: _____

☐ Assignment addresses objective(s)

☐ Enclosed sample provides sufficient evidence

☐ Follow-up conference needed for the following discussion:

_____

_____

_____

_____ Conference held; result:

_____

_____

_____

_____
Reviewed by   Date

Appendix C

Graduate Exit Survey

Directions: For each statement, please indicate the degree to which you agree by selecting 5 strongly agree, 4 agree, 3 no opinion, 2 disagree, or 1 strongly disagree.

Program Goal I. Students identify and demonstrate their levels of computer, information, and technological literacy.

1. I know the basic components of a computer system.   5 4 3 2 1
2. I am knowledgeable about computer operating systems.   5 4 3 2 1
3. I am knowledgeable about software application tools.   5 4 3 2 1
4. I am able to locate, create, analyze, interpret, manage, and use data.   5 4 3 2 1
5. I am knowledgeable about technology.

Program Goal II. Students demonstrate knowledge of communication skills.

6. I can organize a written and an oral message coherently and effectively.   5 4 3 2 1
7. I can use technology for communication.   5 4 3 2 1
8. I know how to research a topic, prepare a report, and present the findings to all organizational levels.   5 4 3 2 1
9. I know how to work in teams.   5 4 3 2 1

Program Goal III. Students demonstrate professional attitudes and conduct.

10. I am ethical in my decision making and behavior.   5 4 3 2 1
11. I can practice professional appearance.   5 4 3 2 1
12. I know acceptable social business behavior.   5 4 3 2 1

Program IV. Students demonstrate global awareness.

13. I am able to apply concepts in a global setting.   5 4 3 2 1
14. I understand cultural differences.   5 4 3 2 1

Program Goal V. Students demonstrate an ability to reflect and to apply critical-thinking skills when solving problems.

15. I can use critical-thinking skills when solving problems.   5 4 3 2 1

16. I can transfer a concept to a specific situation.   5   4   3   2   1
17. I can interpret and synthesize information.   5   4   3   2   1

Program Goal VI. *Students demonstrate and experience real-life applications in a nonacademic environment.*

18. I have observed technological applications in   5   4   3   2   1
    real-life settings.
19. I can apply skills in projects, practicums,   5   4   3   2   1
    internships, and/or student teaching.

Course and Program Assessment Strategies: A Case Study

Susan Jaderstrom
Santa Rosa Junior College, Petaluma Campus
Petaluma, California

The public expects community colleges to be innovative and creative in meeting the needs of the community. Educators are expected to document performance and to be accountable for producing return on taxpayer and student investments. The traditional full-semester course formats no longer meet the needs of the most racially and ethnically diverse student population in our history, a population that is projected to increase in the coming years (McClenny, 1998).

The focus of this chapter is on how Santa Rosa Junior College in Petaluma, California, restructured its educational program to meet the needs of this new student population. In 1995, the enrollment in the business office technology department at the Petaluma campus had dwindled to a handful of students. The college and business community demanded accountability. The instructors and administrators realized that a serious self-assessment of the curriculum, the instructional methods used in the classroom, the contacts with the business community, and the follow-up of graduates must occur.

The decision was made to design certificate programs to meet the needs of students who wanted to quickly enter the job market. The instructors also decided to focus on meeting the entry-level needs of employers. In order to make these changes, closer partnerships with employers were necessary.

A review of literature identified national performance-based intensive training systems. Online search capabilities were used, primarily the Educational Resources Information Center, National Center for Research in Vocational Education, League for Innovation in Community Colleges, and Santa Rosa

Junior College Library article databases. Through these sources, instructors were able to identify and locate examples of competency-based education systems, performance-based assessment techniques, and developments in workforce training in the office technology area.

The Fund for Instructional Improvement sponsored by the Chancellor's Office of the California Community Colleges supported the efforts of Santa Rosa Junior College, Petaluma Campus. The college would conduct research on short-term intensive certificate programs and disseminate the research to other community colleges in California.

Based upon research and self-assessment, and in consultation with local employers, the following changes were made to certificate programs:

- Two semester-length certificates were reduced to eight weeks (12.5 semester units, 240 clock hours of instruction).
- The certificates were renamed Entry-Level Office Worker and Account Clerk.
- The certificate instruction started four weeks after the semester began and ended four weeks before the semester ended.
- Classes were scheduled Monday through Friday, from 9 a.m. to 2:30 p.m. (the hours that children were in school).
- Courses were converted to competency-based instruction determined by employer input. They included only the competencies necessary to obtain entry-level positions.
- The college helped students with job placement for part- and full-time work.
- Follow-up of students was instituted after they successfully completed certificate programs.
- The curriculum was revised as frequently as necessary to meet the demands of business.
- Partnerships were formed with employment agencies and employers.

With the help of a supportive administrator, the instructors in the business office technology department implemented these changes, filled the classes to capacity, and increased enrollment dramatically. In addition, the new certificate programs became a training option for welfare recipients in Sonoma County. In 1995, five certificates were awarded. In 1998, the number of certificates awarded increased to 53.

After implementing the major restructuring of certificates, enrollment has continued to increase, and the graduates are in high demand in the business community. The Board of Governors and Chancellor's Office of the California Community Colleges honored the programs with the Student Success Award for innovative projects and the Shared Dreams Award for the partnerships with county agencies in training welfare recipients.

Preassessment, postassessment, and continual assessments are keys to successful, nontraditional instructional programs.

Assessment Before Starting a Certificate Program

Because classes start at least a month after the traditional semester begins, instructors and counselors have time to meet with prospective students, assess their existing skills, and prepare them for the intensive certificate programs. The following assessments have proven successful.

Orientation meetings. Not all students have the lifestyle, temperament, or learning style that enables them to succeed in an intensive instructional situation. A counselor assigned to the certificate programs coordinates the orientation meetings. The counselor frankly discusses with the students the program pace and stress, study skills, and the need for an organized personal life. This discussion enables students to self-assess whether an intensive certificate program is appropriate for them. The counselor also helps students register for classes and apply for financial aid.

The addition of a counselor to the certificate programs allows instructors to concentrate on teaching, while the counselor provides support for academic and interpersonal issues. The counselor is vitally important for student retention and success.

Hands-on assessment. California community colleges are open-access institutions, which means students cannot be turned away from classes unless the classes have a prerequisite. Since all of the Petaluma campus classes prepare students for entry-level office work, the courses have no prerequisites. During the first two semesters of implementing the certificate programs, instructors realized that students were enrolling with inadequate keyboarding skills or insufficient background in business math and business English.

The OPAC (Office Proficiency and Assessment Certification Program) is used for assessment of keyboarding and 10-key skills. Because OPAC allows the addition of instructor-developed assessments, business math and business English competency tests were written. These assessments were based on analysis of pretest scores and ending competency achievements of 60 students who successfully completed business English and math.

The OPAC software program is available on every computer in the computer laboratory. Therefore, a student can come at any time, take the assessment tests, and determine (with the help of an instructor or counselor) what courses will best prepare him or her for the certificate programs.

Short classes to meet deficiencies. Based upon the OPAC preassessment, students can complete short courses in Introduction to the Computer, Introduction to Microsoft Word, Business Math and Calculator Review, and Business English and Writing Review. These short courses are offered in the month before certificate classes begin. Ninety-six percent of the students who successfully complete the short courses also successfully complete the competencies required for the certificate courses.

Students can also complete self-paced keyboarding, self-paced skill-building, and self-paced 10-key training in the computer lab any time the lab is open. Each self-paced course takes 24 hours to complete.

Workplace Readiness Assessment

Employers in Sonoma County urged instructors to stress to students the importance of attendance and personal responsibility. Based upon this advice, each class in the certificate program (a range of seven to 10 classes) has the same standards for attendance, tardiness, and behavior. The certificate programs have a zero tolerance for absences and inappropriate behavior, and grades are lowered for late work.

After working with a student every day for eight weeks, instructors feel confident telling an employer whether or not the students can take personal responsibility for their attendance and behavior. Some students with personal, child care, substance abuse, or health problems have difficulty meeting the rigor of the certificate programs.

Integration of Competencies in Certificate Courses

According to research by Gonczi and Hager (1994), assessment methods must be capable of measuring competence in an integrated manner. Since students take a daily block of classes for six hours a day, concepts can easily be reinforced from one course into another. If students are not able to apply a concept learned in one class to a similar concept in another class, instructors are able to immediately discover which concepts need further reinforcement. All students use the Internet for research purposes and compose and send e-mail messages in their certificate classes. The following are examples of the integration of competencies.

Business English and Microsoft Word. The instructors work together to integrate concepts learned in each class. For example, when the student learns about the active and passive voice in business English, the Word instructor gives the student a grammar check exercise that assesses this knowledge. In business English, students write letters using proper letter format learned in Word.

Business math and accounting. The same instructor teaches both math and accounting; therefore, it is easy to correlate the competencies learned in one class with the competencies learned in another. Students complete Internet research projects and make group presentations in both classes.

Employment marketing, Microsoft Word, and business English.
Students must use Microsoft Word to prepare grammatically correct and perfectly formatted résumés, cover letters, and thank-you letters.

Business English and communications. Students send e-mail messages
in communications, which are graded not only according to the competencies
learned in business English, but also according to appropriate content.

Examples of Assessment in Courses

Each course uses different assessments, depending upon the subject matter
and method of instruction. The following are examples of course assessment
strategies.

Self-paced courses. Students complete self-paced keyboarding and 10-
key courses on the computer. Keyboarding classes use the ending assessment of
25 words per minute (wpm) for Account Clerks and 35 wpm for Entry-Level
Office Workers (five-minute timing with five or fewer errors). The 10-key class
uses an ending assessment of 9,000 keystrokes per hour with 98 percent accuracy. The temporary agencies recommend the ending keyboarding and 10-key
speeds.

Computer software courses. The assessments for the computer software
courses are the tests available on QUIZ software. QUIZ software is used by
temporary agencies in Sonoma County to assess computer software skills for job
placement.

Employment marketing. All materials prepared for this class must meet
the standard of 100 percent accuracy. The students revise materials until they are
perfect, with points subtracted for each subsequent revision. Students must
submit a résumé (traditional and scannable), cover letter, and employment
application.

In addition, students have one mock interview on campus with an employment specialist and one interview in the community with a potential employer.
Both interviewers complete an evaluation form assessing a student's application
materials, preparation for the interview, and poise during the interview.

Communications. Homework assignments reinforce concepts learned in
class. For example, when studying nonverbal communications, students observe
and record behaviors of their classmates according to information discussed in
class. Students role-play situations whenever possible.

Before students begin telephone training, they job shadow a receptionist in
one of the temporary agencies in the community. Students complete an observation report form and give a brief oral report about their experiences. The

Protocall Telephone Training System allows classroom assessment of skills in answering the telephone and transferring calls. If students' telephone skills do not meet the standard of "excellent," the instructor works with individual students outside of the classroom on improving their telephone techniques.

Students take weekly short-answer quizzes to reinforce their communication and writing skills. The quizzes are graded anonymously in class for immediate feedback.

Word processing. Each day, students learn both Microsoft Word features and proper formatting of office documents. In two hours of hands-on practice immediately following each class, students produce four perfect documents. Two of the assignments have step-by-step instructions, and the other two assignments do not. Students have access to keys to check their work.

Work is graded on proper use of Word features and accurate formatting according to standards of perfection in proofreading and formatting. If the work has more than two minor formatting errors, students are asked to redo the work until it is perfect. The final assessment of the class is a timed test consisting of all the concepts covered in the class. Keys are not available, and the same perfection standards apply, although students are not allowed to retake a test.

Course and Program Assessment

Student assessment. During each class, students have the opportunity to assess how the course is progressing and make recommendations for improvement. If possible, suggestions are immediately implemented. Grades are calculated every two weeks so the students know their class standing at any time. At the conclusion of each certificate program, students complete a thorough assessment of their skills, the classes completed, and the overall certificate program. Students also have the opportunity to meet individually with an instructor for an exit interview at the end of their certificate, which is an opportunity to discuss improvements in the certificate program.

At the conclusion of the certificate programs, the instructors meet, evaluate student and employer recommendations, and make changes to courses or programs. Students consistently indicate that they appreciate the opportunity for input into their educational program and feel pride in seeing their suggestions implemented.

Follow-up statistics. After five semesters of teaching the intensive certificate programs, 250 certificate graduates received follow-up instruments to assess salary data, promotional opportunities, and program satisfaction. The average entry-level wage was $9.81 an hour after eight weeks of training. Survey data indicated that 48 percent of the graduates were promoted within one year, resulting in an average wage of $11.98 an hour. Over 90 percent of the respondents reported "absolutely" or "yes" to whether they were prepared for work after intensive training.

After five semesters of teaching the intensive certificate programs, a comparative analysis was made between regular semester-length courses and intensive courses. The analysis yielded the following data:

- Intensive courses yield performance rates that meet or beat those of regular courses,
- Students enrolled in intensive courses have a higher overall GPA,
- Intensive classes have a higher overall retention rate, and
- Students enrolled in intensive courses have a higher overall successful completion rate.

College Placement Specialist
A placement specialist works with students to find jobs and keeps statistics on wages and student placement data. The specialist also maintains close contact with employers and communicates feedback about courses and graduates, as well as serving on the advisory committee.

Temporary Agencies
A key to successful workforce training is close working relationships with the business community. The instructors have excellent working relationships with all the temporary agencies in Sonoma County. The temporary agencies come to the Employment Marketing class and interview students before graduation. Staff at one of the temporary agencies developed an internship program for certificate graduates. The students work in the employment agency office, their skills are assessed, and then they are placed in temporary jobs at nonprofit organizations.

All the temporary agency employers keep instructors informed about student placements and make recommendations about courses based upon the testing and job placement follow-up of students. Temporary agency employers also participate in the advisory committee.

Recommendations
Specific recommendations from the research on short-term intensive certificate programs completed at Santa Rosa Junior College, Petaluma Campus, include the following:

1. Assess community needs.
2. Know precisely what skills students need to obtain an entry-level job. Base course and program competencies on employer input. Design the curriculum and teaching methods to reflect the work environment.
3. Provide students with an orientation to the demands and expectations of

intensively scheduled programs and courses. An orientation aids students in making appropriate self-assessment about instructional options.

4. Develop models and means to measure competencies. Provide in-class opportunities to demonstrate competencies.
5. Provide support and guidance activities that address students' personal needs, particularly for those students who may be enrolling as a result of welfare reform.
6. Develop a flexible entry/exit system based upon competencies so students can enter the program at the appropriate level or skip courses in which they demonstrate competencies.
7. Develop methods to gather immediate student feedback.
8. Have a strong placement coordinator and partnerships with community employment agencies for placing students in jobs, providing internships, tracking employment, and offering feedback and advice.

Summary

Given the changing business and legislative environments, changing enrollment patterns, and increasing calls for accountability, the future of community colleges should include responsiveness to the needs of the local business community and to the diverse educational goals of students. The program-based intensive training system begins with a community needs assessment. Through the collaboration of innovative, well-trained faculty, competency-based entry-level courses and programs must be developed that not only meet the needs of working and reentry adults, but also meet the demands of the job market.

Program innovations usually involve changing the institutional culture, which is not easy without supportive administrators. The restructuring of an educational program, however, allows instructors to discover a niche market for students. Restructuring also involves constant assessment of students, of courses, and of faculty. This assessment forces instructors to focus on the needs of the students and the community.

The use of a wide variety of assessments has numerous benefits. It not only prepares students for job-placement assessment and on-the-job assessment, but also helps instructors keep course content current and relevant. The employment community rewards hard work and innovation in often unexpected ways such as donations of business clothing; money for scholarships; opportunities for internships; and willingness to serve on advisory committees, speak to students, or teach classes. Colleges reward programs that are accountable with up-to-date equipment and increased funding.

References

Bragg, D. (1996). *Linking college and work: Exemplary policies and practices of two-year college work-based learning programs.* Berkeley, CA: National Center for Research in Vocational Education (NCRVE).

Garrison, D. (1998). Final report, program-based intensive training system. Petaluma, CA: Santa Rosa Junior College, Petaluma Campus.

Gonczi, A., & Hager, P. (1994). General issues about assessment of competence. *Assessment & Evaluation in Higher Education*, (19), 1.

League for Innovation in the Community College. [Online]. Available: http://www.league.org

McCabe, R. H. (Ed.). (1997). *The American community college: Nexus for workforce development.* Mission Viejo, CA: League for Innovation in the Community College.

McClenny, K. M. (1998, August). Community colleges perched at the millennium: Perspectives on innovation, transformation, and tomorrow. *Leadership Abstracts, League for Innovation in the Community College, 11* (8).

McLagan, P. A. (1997, May). Competencies: The next generation. *Training and Development*, 40–47.

National Library of Education, Educational Resources Information Center (ERIC). [Online]. Available: http://www.accesseric.org

National Center for Research in Vocational Education (NCRVE), University of California, Berkeley, CA. [Online]. Available: http://ncrve.berkeley.edu

Nixon, R. O. (1996). *A source document on accelerated courses and programs at accredited two and four year colleges and universities.* Washington, DC: U.S. Department of Education.

Office Proficiency and Assessment Program (OPAC). (Available from Biddle & Associates, Inc., 2100 Northrop Ave., Suite 200, Sacramento, CA 95825, 800-999-0438, ext. 248)

Protocall Telephone Training System. (Available from Square One Groupe, Inc., PO Box 413, St. Joseph, MI 49085, 800-968-7395)

QUIZ Software. (Available from QUIZ Software, 8601 Dunwoody Place, Suite 420, Atlanta, GA 30350, 770-650-8080)

Terry, A. (1984, Winter). Short-term training: A means of providing community colleges and students with long-term benefits. *Community Services Catalyst*, (14) 1.

Authentic Assessment

Ronald F. Fulkert
Eastern Michigan University
Ypsilanti, Michigan

Among the most challenging tasks educators face is assessing student performance. Determining the letter grade a student will receive involves a complex set of decisions. These decisions require evaluation of activities that were performed throughout the semester or grading period and are often influenced by how and where a teacher was trained.

Experts in the field of assessment seem to agree that mere numbers and statistics are not the only variables used when assigning letter grades to students (Benion, 1983; Popham, 1999; and Wiggins, 1993). Wiggins emphasized this point when he stated:

> *Assess the student's accomplishments and progress, not merely the total score that results from points subtracted from a collection of items. In other words, score "longitudinally" toward exemplary performance at exemplary tasks, not by subtraction from "perfection" on simplistic and isolated tests. (p. 171)*

Authentic assessment is one method of evaluation that can help teachers make grading decisions. This assessment strategy has generated much discussion in schools and curricula worldwide. Concerns continue to evolve as to whether students are learning. Administrators use scores on state proficiency-type tests to ensure standards are being met and to evaluate the accountability of teachers. Thomas (1997) stated that "...whether developed at the national or state level, standards must precede and be linked to student tests; for the standards to matter to teachers and students, the test must be based on standards."

Although these tests are designed to evaluate students' skills, knowledge, and abilities, results have been questionable in recent years. As was also reported by Thomas: "One lesson learned with the approach of testing to the standards and holding schools accountable for their students' academic performance was that the process often did not begin positively." However, changing these standardized tests may not be the answer to evaluating learning. Burke described the push for changing state tests as, being "…oversold, and educators will rush to replace one type of flawed standardized test with another type of flawed performance-based test" (1994, p. XV).

As teachers, our primary concern should be, did our students learn the material and achieve the objectives of the course? The answer to this question does not lie in students' abilities to take a paper-and-pencil test. Scores earned on tests simply tell us how well this particular individual can rote learn material concerning a particular topic. For example, psychomotor skills are almost impossible to measure on an objective type test. On essay tests, students may be able to manufacture answers that receive points but do not indicate knowledge, skills, or abilities.

In business education, having students reach higher skill levels is the goal of our teaching. Business education courses depend on an enormous amount of skill and less on rote memory. In Michigan, for example, the Business Services and Technology (BST) programs are performance-based and designed to meet specific standards (Michigan Department of Education, 1994). Students do need to memorize certain concepts and ideas, but teachers in business education expect them to acquire skills and reach competencies in performing tasks.

If business education teachers are interested in ensuring that students are "doers" and possess competencies, then these educators must be open to different methodologies of evaluation. The goal of any business educator should be that their students have learned. Therefore, teachers need to measure "authentic learning." However, Archbald and Newmann (1988) stressed "…that before educators try to assess authentically, they should make sure they teach authentically. Authentic academic achievement is a prerequisite to authentic assessment" (Burke, 1994, p. XV).

To ensure that students have engaged in learning and that teachers have given them the opportunity to achieve higher-order thinking skills, a means to measure this knowledge must transpire. As purported by Burke, Archbald and Newmann suggested " …achievement tasks should meet at least three criteria: disciplined inquiry, integration of knowledge, and value beyond evaluation" (Burke, 1994, p. XV).

Disciplined inquiry in business education depends on students' prior knowledge or an in-depth understanding of a problem. Students are able to formulate new ideas from information input by others. For example, an accounting teacher could give students a worksheet, income statement, and balance sheet and have them write a financial position report for a fiscal period. The students would have to know and make decisions about the relationships among expenses, income, and owner's equity. This process requires the students to think about and solve a given problem for a business.

In this case, students are going far beyond answers to simple questions usually asked on objective style tests and are delivering useful solutions to complex problems introduced by the teacher. This assessment process requires students to use the skills they have learned to arrive at a recommendation that would benefit the business. Students also learn that a problem such as the one illustrated above is closely related to what actually happens in the business world.

Integration of knowledge requires students to consider things as a "whole" rather than as fragments. For business education students, understanding how a spreadsheet would be used to perform financial analysis for a particular company would ensure that the learner knows the value of using Excel. The goal is that students understand why the skills are learned in schools and then how these competencies will be used at work for the rest of their lives.

According to Archbald and Newmann (1988), value beyond evaluation is

> *...when people write letters, news articles, insurance claims, poems; when they speak a foreign language; when they develop blueprints; when they create a painting, a piece of music, or build a stereo cabinet, they demonstrate achievements that have a special value missing in tasks contrived only for the purpose of assessing knowledge (such as spelling quizzes, laboratory exercises, or typical final exams). (p. 3)*

An example in business education may be when students develop a newsletter for parents and friends or assist a local businessperson in developing a database to keep track of clients. Business teachers can use many activities to develop students' skills, knowledge, and abilities in the "value-added arena."

Once a teacher understands the meaning and delivery of "authentic teaching," assessment can be developed. In the teacher education arena, there is an axiom that educators tend to teach the way they were taught. Philosophical beliefs at different universities seem to influence not only the teaching process, but the evaluation procedures as well. Therefore, if change is to occur in education, there must be an aggressive push to inform present teachers that "old methods" may not be the best way to ensure that learning has taken place. Advocating change and approaching assessment with a new mind-set is the primary purpose of this chapter.

Defining and understanding the functions of evaluation are paramount in any formal discussion of how students are judged in regard to being competent in any content area. Two distinctions in evaluation are formative and summative evaluation. How these evaluation processes differ is important in that knowing how an evaluation may be used will influence what is assessed.

Formative Evaluation

Formative evaluation is designed to collect data and information that is used to improve a program or product while the program is still being developed (Dick and Carey, 1996). In that business educators are content specialists, these instructors are ideal candidates to use evaluation of learners to improve instruction. Business teachers do rely somewhat on publishers of textbooks to determine curriculum, but students can assist these educators much more in designing meaningful activities through formative-type evaluation.

For example, if classes are taught in Microsoft PowerPoint, students can be evaluated on the effectiveness of a slide show being used as part of a presentation in another content area. After the assessment, the teacher may add or change parts of the instruction in PowerPoint where students' evaluations indicated confusion or misunderstanding.

Business educators are constantly using the feedback from students' evaluations to improve instruction. Popham stated that teachers "do their own formative evaluations because they wish to spruce up their instruction" (1999, p. 299). Unfortunately, there are educators who teach courses semester after semester with very little or no change in the curriculum. These are the teachers who try to put their classes on "autopilot" and assume learning will take place. Wong and Wong refer to these teachers as those who are on survival status (1996).

Learners today are becoming more sophisticated and involved in the process of their education; and they challenge teachers if the instruction becomes boring and unrelated to "real-world" experiences. Fortunately, for today's learners, more teachers are using formative evaluation in conjunction with "authentic type" assessments to improve curriculum and methodologies of teaching.

Technological improvements and upgrades have also forced business educators to change more frequently than if technology remained static. For example, both the Microsoft and Corel Suites programs have had numerous upgrades in the last five years. To keep up, business educators must change their curriculums.

Summative Evaluation

Summative evaluation is used after an instructional program has been implemented and formative evaluation completed. "The purpose is to present conclusions about the worth of the program or product and make recommenda-tions about its adoption or retention" (Dick and Carey, 1996, p. 348). According to Popham, teachers may be called on to supply evidence (such as students' test results) then may use this evidence for accountability purposes (1999).

Administrators can also use these summative evaluations to support the notion that teachers' course objectives are being met, students' achievements are within the range of expectations, parents are informed of activities within a classroom, and teachers are promoted or receive tenure (Popham, 1999).

Authentic Assessment

Effective assessment begins with clear goals and objectives. The first assessment cannot take place until all students are aware of exactly what they are supposed to know upon completion of any class or lesson. Methods classes at universities try to prepare students to understand just how important behavioral objectives are to the teaching process. Objectives drive the lesson and must be stated in detail so unit and lesson plans can be developed.

Once a teacher has decided what students need to know upon completion of the lesson, choices can be made as to how to assess their knowledge. This process is where authentic assessment becomes a valuable tool for the teacher. Alternatives to conventional, objective, multiple-choice testing are frequently referred to as alternative assessment, authentic assessment, and performance-based assessment and are sometimes used synonymously. These synonyms, according to Herman, Aschbacher, and Winters, are descriptors used to identify a process in which students are required to generate rather than choose a response (1992).

Deciding on the method of assessing students can be a trying task for any educator. Benion emphasizes the notion that a teacher should labor in the development of a self-designed test and then use that assessment instrument as a learning opportunity. Development of objective tests is usually not given the time required by teachers to ensure that the instruments are reliable and valid (Benion, 1983). Therefore, an alternative method of assessing students may be more beneficial for the students and teacher.

Zeliff and Schultz have stated that "… projects, presentations, and portfo-lios are examples of performance and authentic assessment" (1996, p. 87). Several other assessment tools used in business education, such as personal journals, conferences, and interviews, are gaining attention in education circles (Burke, 1994). These authentic assessment tools (projects, modules, presenta-tions, portfolios, personal journals, interviews, and conferences) make good substitutes for traditional objective tests and each may be designed to evaluate students' achievement or competencies in a unique manner. Each will be discussed in detail later.

Designing an Instrument

Prior to designing any learning activity, the teacher must decide how the student will be evaluated and how much an exercise will count toward the final grade. B. E. Walvoord suggested that "... the more explicit a teacher is in the explanation of how an item will be graded the higher the caliber of work" (oral communication, Eastern Michigan University Workshop, February 5, 1999). Her recommendation was to develop a rubric or a primary trait analysis. These structured guides require great detail so students become aware of exactly what they must do to receive all of the points for any given activity.

While Walvoord emphasized that teachers must be extremely explicit in their directions of how the work will be evaluated, these ideas are not taught in every university across the country. Foran, Pucel, Fruehling, and Johnson cautioned designers of assessment instruments to keep in mind that errors are an integral part of evaluation. Therefore, controls must be established to guard against (a) student error, (b) instrument error, (c) guessing error, and (d) scorer error (1990). Using rubrics should help the teacher in controlling these errors.

According to Berry, "a rubric is a written guide/criteria by which performance/product/process is judged by means of a peer review process, instructor assessment, and/or self-assessment. It may not be the end result. A rubric may serve as an analysis, requiring one to look back at what was assessed and reflect on what was learned" (Michigan Department of Education, 1994, p. 10). Rubrics will provide the student with input to achieve or maximize learning by

- Showing the best work and expectations based on modules,
- Providing a profile for the best work,
- Establishing ideal-learner goals,
- Providing clear directions and focus for learning/relearning and teaching and reteaching,
- Allowing for divergence and range (acting like a gauge), and
- Creating feedback loops (Berry, 1997).

Walvoord defined primary trait analysis (PTA) as (oral communication with author, February 5, 1999)

- A method of explicitly stating the criteria for evaluation of a performance;
- Assignment specific; for each performance, the assessor builds a unique set of criteria;
- A way to identify the factors or "traits" that will count for the scoring (e.g. thesis, materials and methods, use of color, eye contact with client), which then builds a scale for scoring the student's performance with each trait.

Whether a teacher decides to use the term rubric or primary trait analysis is not important, but the students must be informed of the scale used for evaluation.

Suggestions for developing a PTA according to Walvoord are

1. Choose a test or assignment that tests central goals/objectives of the course.
2. Identify the factors or "traits" that will "count" in the assessment. These are nouns (e.g. thesis, eye contact with client, use of color, control of variables).
3. For each trait, construct a 3–5-point scale. These are descriptive statements (e.g. a "5" thesis is limited enough to treat within the scope of the essay and is clear to the reader; it enters the dialogue of the discipline as reflected by the student's sources, and it does so at a level that shows synthesis and original thought; it neither exactly repeats any of the student's sources nor states the obvious).
4. Go over the scale with a colleague and revise.
5. Try out the scale with student work and revise.
6. Teach a colleague to use the scale, check inter-rater reliability, and revise.

Once students understand exactly what the teacher is evaluating, they can compile information and perform the tasks. Furthermore, students will be less likely to miss items if they are aware points will be deducted for not including such items within any given activity. Naturally, the PTA is incorporated to meet the objective established to achieve competencies for any given activity. Table 1 illustrates an objective and a corresponding PTA for assessment.

Table 1. Personal Business Letter

Objective: Given a lecture on how to design and type a personal business letter, the student will be able to use touch-keyboarding and word processing skills to produce a personal business letter with 80 percent accuracy. (Maximum 50 points)

Trait: Uses proper formatting, grammar, and style to produce a personal business letter accurately and in a timely fashion.

	Good				Poor
Recognizing and Correcting Errors					
Formatting	5	4	3	2	1
Grammar	5	4	3	2	1
Spelling	5	4	3	2	1
Capitalization	5	4	3	2	1
Punctuation	5	4	3	2	1
Word usage	5	4	3	2	1
Misstrokes	5	4	3	2	1
Time Management					
No extra keystrokes	5	4	3	2	1
Document produced within the given time limit	5	4	3	2	1
Keyboarding Skills					
Proper technique	5	4	3	2	1

Even though there is a very explicit number to judge each particular competency, the teacher must still make objective decisions. A rubric or PTA can be used to evaluate all authentic tools. Angelo and Cross emphasized the fact that if students are given an opportunity to participate in the development of an assessment instrument, such as a rubric or performance task analysis, faculty and students working together can achieve better results and appreciate greater value in achievement (1993). Students can also experience satisfaction and become aware of a shared goal of improved learning. As with any concept or idea in education, there is always a flip side or negative aspect that must be considered when trying new methods.

According to experts in the field of student assessment, one of the greatest disadvantages of using a rubric, PTA, or any other explicit instrument is that it requires a substantial amount of time to develop (Burke, 1994; Walvoord, 1999; Zeliff and Schultz, 1996). More specifically to business education, Zeliff and Schultz state: "Rubrics take time to develop, and few examples exist for the business curriculum. Instructors must determine criteria, descriptors, and formatting; if the assignment is new or being revised, the instructor must take time to design the lesson and its rubric" (1996, p. 103).

Walvoord was also concerned with when to share the evaluation instrument with students. She emphasized that if students are made aware of exactly what the assessor is looking for when grading, learners usually "cover the material, and do a good job meeting the objective of the unit or lesson" (1999). Using a very explicit design to assess students' work is worth the teachers' time required in the construction of an evaluation tool.

Projects

The myriad of projects being used today in business education requires teachers to use innovative measures to ensure that students are getting credit for knowledge, skills, and abilities gained in the classroom. Business partners and advisory committees are insisting that education mimic the corporate world so that students gain expertise in problem solving, group processing, and reasoning. One popular style of project used in many business education classes is modules.

Modules

Modules fit the agenda being requested by the business partners and advisory committees. In addition, students appear to like the idea of being able to work independently. Many teachers in the field use modules to give some of the advanced students an opportunity to take on the roles of mentors, group leaders, or teaching assistants. These roles require the leadership knowledge, skills, and abilities corporations are looking for in business education graduates.

Modules can be divided into small segments that require a short time to complete or advanced packages that take a week or two to finish. Calhoun and Robinson emphasized that higher cognitive learning occurs in classrooms where the teacher becomes a facilitator and students work independently or in a group on projects. These environments resemble offices in the business sector; students are busy accomplishing required tasks just like their counterparts in many local companies (1995).

Using modules and projects makes the student transition from school to work less stressful. Some basic guidelines for developing a module include the following:

- Indicate expected outcomes (performance objective).
- Give directions for the module (sometimes referred to as a demonstration mountain) starting at the bottom and working toward the top.
- Describe in the teacher's notes what the students will do.
- Give rubrics—
  1. Product rubric (evaluation of the product) and
  2. Process rubric (evaluation of the procedures).
- Look at the skill competencies for the component that is being written.
- Decide which skill should be covered in the module.
- Create a student scenario whereby these skills will be demonstrated.
- Create smaller modules to be used at first to help build students' confidence.

Tables 2 through 5 are examples for establishing a module and then assessing the skills students have learned.

Table 2. Module for Content Goal
A. Instruction topic
B. Prerequisite(s)—specific competencies
C. Directions for module
D. Interest approach
E. Performance objectives
F. Preassessment—if there is none, this must be stated
G. Learning experience
H. Subgoal topic
I. Posttest
J. References and resources

Table 3. Lesson Plan for Content Goal

Answering the Telephone

Instructional Topic

Displaying telephone etiquette

Prerequisites

None

Interest Approach (Time: 15 minutes)

The teacher will role-play answering the telephone in a variety of negative and positive ways.

Performance Objective

The student will display telephone etiquette. Performance will be satisfactory if all the goals on the following checklist are met.

Preassessment

Starting Point Pretest (Time: 0 minutes)

No starting point test. The instructional approach begins at ground level.

Exemption Test

No exemption test is offered.

Learning Experiences

Subgoal Topic: Demonstrate skill in providing and obtaining information

Domain: Affective

Level: Awareness

Theory of Learning: Association

Method of Delivery: Lecture/Presentation (Time: 30 minutes)

Instructor Practices

1. Teacher will discuss the positive and negative effects of answering the telephone on the image of a company.
2. Teacher will give handout and telephone booklet listing ways to place and accept calls.

Assignments (Time: 60 minutes)

1. The student will role-play providing and obtaining information.
2. The student will evaluate the role-playing activity from #1.

Posttest (Time: 10 minutes)

A production test will be administered. Students will be tape-recorded, and a video will be made of students for detailed assessment of their skills.

Table 4. Process Rubric

Telephone Skills

Quality is expected.

Quality will be measured.

The business is professionally represented when the telephone is answered with courtesy, and an accurate message is communicated and conveyed.

To perform quality telephoning a student must

- Utilize telephone courtesy,
- Practice telephone etiquette,
- Answer incoming calls,
- Make outgoing calls,
- Take accurate messages, and
- Handle multi-line telephones.

Table 5. Product Rubric

Telephone Skills

Evaluation ratings (points may be awarded for each category at the discretion of the teacher to allocate sufficient points for the activity).

WC = World Class: tasks done correctly the first time.

HC = Highly Competent: tasks need prompting or have minor deviations.

RV = Needs Revision: tasks need to be completed or need more than minor revisions.

Self-Directed Learner

Learners create a positive vision for themselves and their futures, set priorities and achievable goals, create options for themselves, monitor and evaluate their programs, and assume responsibility for themselves.

	WC	HC	RV
Completes assessment within time guidelines			
Needs no prompting to complete assessment			
Needs no outside assistance to complete assessment			

Collaborative Contributor

Uses effective leadership and group skills to develop and manage interpersonal relationships within diverse settings.

Table 5. Product Rubric (contd.)

	WC	HC	RV
Works as a team member to communicate			

Effective Communicator

Reads, listens, analyzes, interprets, and responds in order to convey significant messages to others and to receive, interpret, and utilize the messages of others.

	WC	HC	RV
Uses visual aids			
Uses verbal communication			
Uses written communication			

Total points acquired _____

Total points possible _____

Adapted from PEAK Learning Systems, Inc. (Sparks and Ziehm, 1997)

Presentations

Technological advances have led instructors to require more student presentations. Microsoft PowerPoint, Lotus Freelance, Corel Presentation, and other software packages have made presenting material to a group easier and more effective. If a student uses the outline feature of PowerPoint, the efficiency should increase because of the step-by-step process that the software requires to prepare the slide show.

Evaluations of presentations can be accomplished in two different categories: (a) the preparation of the slide show (product rubric) and (b) the actual oral delivery (process rubric). The evaluations can also be made using one rubric or PTA that has been divided into two parts.

In addition to knowing the technical skills necessary to perform PowerPoint applications, students are required to apply this knowledge to a personal or hypothetical situation that exercises such higher-order thinking skills as reasoning, evaluation, problem solving, and decision making. Students will use creative thinking to develop the purpose of the application, reasoning and problem solving to analyze the appropriate use of technology, and evaluation to apply and test features of the software. They will be required to create slides that are appropriate to support the presentation, use clip art and transitions to encourage the audience to participate, and summarize and make recommendations in the oral report. An example is given in Table 6.

After the primary trait score matrix is prepared, the teacher can easily adapt the guide to evaluate the activity for a weight that is reasonable for the material. For example, the above exercise could use a multiple factor of four to

Table 6. PowerPoint Presentation and Oral Report

Trait: Identifies the purpose of the application in the introduction.

5	4	3	2	1
Identifies the topic of the presentation, goals and objectives, and how the application will be used.	Identifies the topic of the presentation and goals and objectives.	Identifies the purpose of the presentation.	Purpose of the presentation is unclear.	Fails to identify the purpose of the presentation.

Trait: Uses the PowerPoint application in a logical format, integrates appropriate clip art, and follows proper grammar and communication rules to support the report.

5	4	3	2	1
Based on chosen application, student constructs a PowerPoint presentation in a clearly understood format using appropriate slides (at least 10) and clip art (at least 3 pieces). Includes transitions, builds, and creativity.	Based on chosen application, student constructs a PowerPoint presentation in a clearly understood format using appropriate slides (at least 10) and clip art (at least 3 pieces).	Based on chosen application, student constructs a PowerPoint presentation in a logical format using appropriate slides.	Based on chosen application, student constructs a PowerPoint presentation in unclear, illogical format and does not use appropriate slides or clip art.	PowerPoint presentation is based on an application that is not logically or clearly understood by the audience.

determine the total number of points available for the activity. In this case, a factor of four would make the total activity worth 40 points—20 points for content and 20 points for presentation. This process gives students a clear, specific, and precise scale that will be used to measure achievement. Students know the target, usually achieve higher scores, and complete quality work.

Portfolios

Popham gives a very explicit definition and introduction to the concept of using portfolios for the purpose of assessing students. He states,

> In education, portfolios refer to a systematic collection of one's work. Although the application of portfolios in education has been

a relatively recent phenomenon, portfolios have been widely used in
a number of other fields for many years. Portfolios, in fact, consti-
tute the chief method by which certain professionals display their
skills and accomplishments. For example, portfolios are tradition-
ally used for that purpose by photographers, artists, journalists,
models, architects, and so on. An important feature of portfolios is
that they must be updated as a person's achievements and skills
grow. (1999, p. 181)

Portfolios take on many different shapes and sizes: files, folders, notebooks, boxes, videos, computer disks, and CD-ROMs. They require synthesis
and creative thinking. The process of developing a portfolio gives students the
opportunity to express exactly what they have been learning in any situation. For
example, student teachers develop and design portfolios to demonstrate their
learning during the internship.

Many experts in the field of education support the notion that portfolios
can be used as

- Tools for discussion with peers, teachers, and parents;
- Vehicles for students to demonstrate their skills and understanding;
- Opportunities to set future goals;
- Documentation of students' development and growth in ability, attitudes,
  and expression;
- Demonstrations of different learning styles, multiple intelligences, and
  cultural diversity;
- Occasions for students to make critical choices about what they select for
  their portfolios;
- Tools for students to trace the development of their learning; and
- Opportunities for students to make connections between prior knowledge
  and new learning (Burke, 1994, p. 45).

Many advocates of portfolios believe that assessment using portfolios will
develop good relationships between teachers and students. These advocates also
stress that such instruments can be used as formative or summative evaluation
devices, and can be used as lifelong learning tools. Employing portfolios as
assessment tools requires dedicated time by teachers, but measures outcomes in
ways that they could not be assessed by any other evaluation instrument. The list
of differences in portfolio assessment versus testing is lengthy; however, two
major differences are (a) portfolios link assessment and teaching to learning
whereas testing separates learning, testing, and teaching, and (b) portfolios have
a goal of student self-assessment whereas testing does not have a goal of self-
assessment. As cited in Popham (1999) and in Farr and Tone (1994), the real
payoff from proper portfolio assessment is that students' self-evaluation capabilities are enhanced.

Rubrics and PTA can be used in portfolio assessment just as they can be used with any other evaluation tool. Criteria must be established prior to the assignment so students will know exactly what to do to receive an acceptable grade. The diverseness of a portfolio can lead to a number of options. For example, the teacher may decide

- Not to grade the portfolio but to assess whether the "work is acceptable";
- To grade the overall presentation and assign a point value for the entire work;
- To grade selected pieces, using predetermined criteria;
- To post selected entries on bulletin boards (especially for open houses); and
- To use the portfolio for other activities, such as interviews or journal entries.

As with other assessments, a rubric grid would be developed to ensure all parts were included. For example, the teacher informs students that their portfolios must include the following items:

- A letter of introduction;
- A table of contents;
- Identification of the skills or knowledge being demonstrated;
- A sample of homework;
- Dates on all entries;
- A copy of the rubric being used;
- The student's self-reflection on all entries; and
- Neatness, clarity, and overall design.

A checkoff style rubric could be developed as illustrated in Table 7.

Table 7. Portfolio Checklist

Element	Exceeds Expectations (3)	Meets Expectations (2)	Does Not Meet Expectations (1)	Total
Letter of introduction				
Table of contents				
Identification of skills				
Samples of homework				
Dates on all entries				
Copy of rubric				
Self-reflection on entries				
Quality (neatness, etc.)				

An essential element that business education teachers must realize and maintain in portfolio assessment is that it is an ongoing process meant to help them judge students' progress and growth. Many teachers have become proponents of student portfolios. These instruments take an extraordinary amount of time to prepare and grade compared to objective tests.

Some experts argue, however, that portfolios used for employees are not as popular as they appear. At a seminar, a group of human resource managers emphasized unanimously that "portfolios may be ideal for hiring certain types of employees such as models, artists, or architects, but businesses in general do not have the time to view portfolios" (oral communication, Eastern Michigan University, Summer Institute, June 27, 1997). Whether or not the portfolio is used for employment, the teachers should still implement exercises and activities that use the portfolio to build skills for students.

Personal Journals

"Learning logs and reflective journals have been used by teachers as formative or ongoing assessment tools for years, but, unfortunately, mostly by teachers of English" (Burke, 1994, p. 84). This type of assessment tool can also benefit business education teachers. Implementing the use of personal journals or learning logs gives students another opportunity to use creative writing integrated with problem solving, leadership, synthesis thinking, and other skills desired by the corporate world.

The axiom that students need to express themselves in today's learning environment could not be truer in business education classes. These journals or learning logs give students the opportunity to recognize their own strengths and weaknesses (Angelo and Cross, 1993). This opportunity for acquiring self-knowledge coupled with teachers' ability to evaluate students' skills will produce a higher level of involvement by learners.

Teachers who use personal journals as a learning tool must inform the students up front that any comments written in the log will remain private (unless some threatening, pornographic, or other undesirable comment is made). Students need to know that they can share inner thoughts without risking criticism. Many students will have little experience creating journals; therefore, explicit detail of what the teacher wants and expects is paramount during the introductory phase of using personal journals.

Journals will give the teacher an indication that there is confusion about a topic if more than a handful of students express misunderstanding. Students tend to enjoy this style of assessment because they feel less bothered by the process than they do by studying for and taking a paper-and-pencil test. Students often spend more time writing in a journal than reading and preparing for a test.

Using journals and logs for assessment is similar to using portfolios. The process employed depends on the individual teacher and the nature of the assignment. Some suggestions are

- Teachers should evaluate using a continuum.
- Journals should involve a level of thoughtfulness.
- Teachers can assign point values for logs and journals.
- A Likert scale can be used to assess journals.
- Students can turn in journals on a periodic basis for feedback or a grade. The grade can be based on the number of entries (based on predetermined criteria) or a combination of quality and quantity.
- Students can share a journal with a partner or cooperative group. Peers can provide oral feedback and assign a grade based on predetermined criteria.
- Students can complete a self-assessment of their journal entries based on predetermined criteria.
- Teachers can choose random entries to be graded or included in a student's portfolio (Burke, 1994).

Journals and learning logs can be very successful assessment tools; however, some students are too tough on themselves and have difficulty with self-assessment. In addition, students may spend entirely too much time concentrating on their weaknesses rather than their strengths. Overall, however, the time required to use journals for a portion of a grade is worthwhile.

Interviews and Conferences

Teachers often use interviews during employability skills units, but personal communications can also be used for evaluating a multitude of competencies. Even though using interviews for evaluation and grading is beneficial to the student, teachers are often reluctant to implement direct personal communication as an assessment tool because this technique relies on substantial subjectivity.

Business partners and advisory committees continue to encourage teachers to integrate oral communications into the curriculum of business education programs. The use of interviews for assessment gives business students an excellent opportunity to exchange ideas and thoughts through oral communications. Besides during assessment activities, students should be encouraged to communicate with their peers at an acceptable business level every day.

Peer interviews are ideal for helping students develop and practice good interviewing techniques. The list of activities that could be assessed orally is endless. If teachers use structured interviews in the classroom, students will benefit from this practice when they begin to look for a job. Employers today rely heavily on how well potential employees interview.

Structured interviews also give teachers the opportunity to collect information about students across different time periods, allowing for learner improvement. According to Burke, interviews enable teachers to collect information in a way that cannot be gathered in any other manner (1994). These interviews also give students the opportunity to use their higher-order thinking skills. Students may find structured interviews

- Help clarify thinking,
- Assist in reflection about their own learning,
- Help them achieve new levels of understanding,
- Facilitate self-evaluation,
- Make them feel their ideas and opinions are valued,
- Help them appreciate progress and set future goals,
- Allow them to respond to teacher comments,
- Build positive teacher-student relationships, and
- Lead them to become self-directed learners (Burke, 1994, p. 130).

The criteria that could be used for assessing personal interviews are very broad and generic. Competencies a teacher would want to evaluate include

- Proper use of English grammar,
- Poise and mannerisms,
- Body language,
- Content and directness of answers, and
- Listening and interpretation of questions.

Table 8 illustrates a checkoff style rubric for assessing an interview.

Table 8. Interview

Task	Exemplary	Acceptable	Needs Work
Proper introduction			
Voice (enthusiasm, volume)			
Platform (gesture, eye contact)			
Organization (logical, clearly understood, suitable to topic)			
Content (development of subject, depth of research)			
Mechanics (diction, grammar)			
Closing (summary, conclusion)			
Effectiveness (purpose achieved)			
		Total points	

*Scoring Guide: Exemplary 10 , Acceptable 8, Needs Work 6

Summary

Authentic assessment is growing in popularity and will continue to grow, if teachers use projects, presentations, portfolios, and interviews to evaluate students' skills. Teachers must change their methods of evaluating students to incorporate these new strategies. Rote learning and memorization are not designed to measure the knowledge, skills, and attitudes that industry is demanding of our students. Educational experts and advisory committees are insisting that business classes mimic the "real world." If teachers use evaluation activities that mirror the types of assessment designs used by employers, students will develop the higher-order thinking skills desired by industry.

As teachers become more familiar with using authentic assessment tools to evaluate students, less time will be spent designing rubrics and PTA. Students will benefit when they know exactly how they are going to be evaluated; and their interest in classes and grades will increase. The idea of motivating learners should encourage all teachers to implement authentic assessment.

References

Angelo, T. A., & Cross, K. P. (1993). *Classroom assessment techniques: A handbook for college teachers.* San Francisco: Jossey-Bass Inc., Publishers.

Archbald, D. A., & Newmann, F. M. (1988). *Beyond standardized testing: Assessing authentic academic achievement in the secondary school.* Madison, WI: University of Wisconsin and National Association of Secondary School Principals.

Benion, D. H. (1983). *Assessing student learning.* Garden City Park, NY: Avery Publishing.

Berry, J. (1997). Business services and technology (BST) examples and modules. Ypsilanti, MI: Michigan Department of Education.

Burke, K. (1994). *The mindful school: How to assess authentic learning,* (Rev. ed.). Arlington Heights, IL: Skylight Training and Publishing, Inc.

Calhoun, C. C., & Robinson, B. W. (1995). *Managing the learning process in business education.* Birmingham, AL: Colonial Press.

Dick, W., & Carey, L. (1996). *The systematic design of instruction* (4th ed.). New York: Harper Collins College.

Farr, R. C., & Tone, B. (1994). The portfolio and performance assessment: Helping students evaluate their progress as readers and writers. In *Growing to meet your needs.* New York: Harcourt Brace College Publishers.

Foran, J. V., Pucel, D. J., Fruehling, R. T., & Johnson, J. C. (1990). *Effective curriculum planning: Performances, standards, and outcomes.* St. Paul, MN: Paradigm.

Herman, J. L., Aschbacher, P. R, & Winters, L. (1992). *A practical guide to alternative assessment.* Alexandria, VA: Association for Supervision and Curriculum Development.

Michigan Department of Education. (1994). *Standards culminating activities and assessment instruments.* Lansing, MI: Michigan State University.

Popham, W. J. (1999). *Classroom assessment: What teachers need to know.* Boston: Allyn and Bacon.

Sparks, K., & Ziehm, J. (1997). Answering the telephone. *Curriculum in BST.* Ypsilanti, MI: Eastern Michigan University.

Thomas, T. P. (1997). Using standards to make a difference: Four options. *Educational Horizons, 75* (3), 121–125.

Walvoord, B. E. (1999, February 5). Eastern Michigan University Workshop, Ypsilanti, Michigan.

Wiggins, G. P. (1993). *Assessing student performance: Exploring the purpose and limits of testing.* San Francisco: Jossey-Bass Inc., Publishers.

Wong, H. K., & Wong, R. T. (1996). *The effective teacher.* Mountain View, CA: Harry K. Wong Publications, Inc.

Zeliff, N. D., & Schultz, K. A. (1996). Authentic assessment. In H. R. Perreault (Ed.), *Classroom strategies: The methodology of business education, 1996 NBEA Yearbook* (No. 34, pp. 87–105). Reston, VA: National Business Education Association.

Alternative Assessment

Nancy D. Zeliff
Northwest Missouri State University
Maryville, Missouri

The *National Standards for Business Education* (1995) and state frame-works guide the business curriculum relative to what students should know and be able to accomplish. But how do we evaluate students reaching these compe-tencies? Traditional assessment in the form of objective examinations accurately measures lower-level cognitive skills such as factual recall and comprehension. To measure higher-level cognitive skills and the affective domain, as well as the general attainment of skills and knowledge with more validity, alternative assessment strategies must be employed.

Assessment has several objectives. Monitoring student progress and achievement remains its primary purpose. Other purposes include assisting in program evaluation, reviewing curriculum, improving instruction, and assessing teacher effectiveness. It is evident that a "paper-and-pencil" traditional test cannot adequately meet these purposes of assessment and that additional methods must be used. This chapter will discuss learning activities and suitable alternative assessment strategies, the diversity of learners and how alternative assessment can better evaluate these learners, the development of checklists and scoring guides (rubrics), and alternative delivery systems, such as Web-based learning, that demand new testing protocols.

Diverse Learners

Attention to diversity is important because of changing demographics and the value of diversity in business (McEwen and McEwen, 1996). Women, minorities, and immigrants already comprise a greater portion of today's workforce. The census of 2000 will undoubtedly reveal additional diversity shifts in the U.S. population. Diversity includes physical disabilities, educational levels, learning styles, academic levels, gender, age, religion, and cultural backgrounds (Ownby and Perreault, 1994).

Because all learners are not alike, a combination of traditional and alternative assessment can provide a broader scope of opportunities for students to demonstrate what they know. The differences that affect learning most are academic levels and learning styles. If all assessments are administered through writing, students with poorer language arts skills and lower reading levels will not perform to their optimum. Students who learn primarily through kinesthetic or hands-on methods would also not perform at their best through written examinations.

Alternative assessment methods, such as interviews, observation, or portfolios, which utilize less reading/writing and more demonstration and performance, would provide a more accurate assessment of student progress and achievement. The key to assessment of learners, programs, and teachers is utilizing multiple assessments that are both valid and reliable.

Valid strategies assess what was intended to be measured. A valid method of evaluating a student's ability to prepare a business letter, for example, is to have the learner format such a document. A less valid method is to administer a quiz of 10 objective questions about formatting business letters. Validity is often increased when performance assessments are used.

Reliable assessments measure consistently when the student both repeats the assessment and performs the same on each, and when multiple evaluators consistently judge student competence. Traditional objective examinations are more reliable measures than performance assessments are. But reliability is increased with performance assessment when multiple evaluators use observation checklists or scoring guides (rubrics) that list the expected traits and behaviors of the students.

McEwen and McEwen (1996) identified varied types of assessment that would be appropriate in accurately assessing student progress and achievement for diverse learners:

- Essay questions that allow for justification and discussion,
- Oral reports by small groups,
- Portfolios of students' work over time,
- Observations of students working individually or in groups,
- Peer evaluation, and
- Videotaped performances of students' work completed in their "comfort zones."

Alternative Assessment Strategies

Three categories of alternative assessment strategies—process, written, and portfolios—are detailed in Table 1 (Zeliff and Schultz, 1998).

Table 1. Alternative Assessment

Process	Written	Portfolios
Anecdotal	Essays	Course
Observation checklist	Case studies	Career
Evaluation	Reflections	District
Peer	Journals	
Self	Class notebooks	
Interviews	Logs	
Demonstrations	Reading	
	Writing	
	Learning	

Process. Process assessment emphasizes the manner in which students complete the task. The final result is secondary. One process method of assessment is an anecdotal record compiled by the evaluator while observing a student completing a task. Reliability is enhanced when the process is observed repeatedly by the same evaluator or by multiple evaluators. Anecdotal records assess student progress over time. Hands-on activities or skills that can be effectively evaluated by anecdotal records are troubleshooting hardware, delivering customer service, and operating business machines.

An observation checklist is commonly used in business education in process evaluation and is more reliable than an anecdotal record. Keyboarding technique is often measured by a checklist that the evaluator uses to determine the student's keystroking, posture, and "eyes on copy." The checklist is more reliable than anecdotal records because expected traits and behaviors are listed and frequencies of these traits and behaviors can be recorded. When the checklist is shared with students in advance of the observation, the criteria by which they will be evaluated are known and can guide their improvement.

Peer and self-evaluation, peer contributions and observations, and student self-reflection are useful methods for providing specific feedback to the teacher about the learning activity. Peer evaluation offers insight into an individual's contributions to the group process and finished product. When small groups are used in the classroom, it is impossible for the evaluator to observe all groups simultaneously. Therefore, peer evaluation provides helpful cues relative to the part each group member played. Peer evaluation of an individual's work or performance also brings constructive and often empathetic views not experienced by the teacher. Self-evaluation brings reflection to the learning process and can be done with journal entries or student responses to teacher-directed questions.

Group work is often completed in business classrooms with collaborative projects such as research presentations, Web page development, and mock trials. The finished products of the research findings, Web page, and trial outcome can be assessed by other means, but to identify how much and how well group members contributed and what the student learned, peer and self-evaluation is needed. Diverse learners benefit from group projects by contributing their strengths to the group effort and reaping the strengths of other group members.

Interviews are useful evaluation methods for all learners and help promote the development of oral communication skills. This assessment technique, however, is especially beneficial with students who have a physical disability that makes writing laborious or impossible or a learning disability that makes composing written responses difficult. All students should be asked the same questions, and responses should be recorded on a checklist or other evaluation instrument to maintain reliability. Interviews are effective assessments to evaluate peers involved in group work or to gain learner feedback on speakers or field trips.

Competence in a skill or process can be clearly observed in a demonstration. This assessment method is highly valid in measuring a skill or knowledge. Tasks in a business classroom that are best assessed by demonstration include 10-key skills on a numeric keypad and computer application tasks such as copying files and copying/pasting text. Reliability in observing the demonstration is increased when the evaluator uses predetermined criteria. Diverse learners may need more time to demonstrate their skill or need to repeat the demonstration until mastery is achieved.

Written. Written assessments are valid for measuring higher-level cognitive skills and knowledge, as well as written communication skills. Learners can respond in writing through essays or reaction papers about current business events. Those with learning disabilities in language arts, however, will find such assessments more difficult. Extending time, offering a teacher example, or providing other language arts assistance will reduce fear and dread of written assessments among these learners.

Students with a language other than English as their dominant language (ESL learners) may also need more time and should be allowed to use translation dictionaries and other reference assistance. When they are allowed to combine another assessment technique such as interviewing with written exercises, these learners can excel with the interview to compensate for the difficulty usually found in written examinations. The use of a scoring guide (rubric) or checklist increases the reliability of written assessment strategies.

A case study is a type of assessment that presents a situation to the learner and is typically found in the business law classroom. Students must respond by justifying the stated outcome and applying previous knowledge. Actual case studies from business situations can be used to add authenticity to the learning and evaluation process. To meet the needs of diverse learners, educators should allow for the results of case studies to be orally presented at times and in writing at other times.

Reflections written by students are usually not graded but provide valuable information to both the learner and the evaluator. Without the pressure of grades, all students are generally encouraged to write more truthfully and freely about their learning and their reaction to the class activity. Reflections are not only helpful to the learner but offer valuable feedback to the evaluator, as well, and are appropriate to require of students after a performance such as a job interview or oral presentation.

Journal entries can include student reflection and also serve as a chrono-logical record of learning and tasks completed. Entries can be especially useful with group projects in business classes when used to record group meetings outside of class and responsibilities assumed by each group member. Groups typically include diverse learners of different academic levels, gender, socioeco-nomic groups, and cultural and ethnic backgrounds.

Class notebooks or portfolios are used to compile course materials and written notes and to provide students with an organizational tool. Such a system helps instill resource management and organizational skills in learners, especially those with Attention Deficit Disorder. In a keyboarding class, learners could place in their class notebook documents prepared throughout the course, timed writing records, and class notes.

Notebooks are also helpful to students in high-stakes assessments and enable them to maintain, synthesize, and review information in preparing for these important evaluations. High-stakes assessment measures include profes-sional certification exams (state boards, bar exam, PRAXIS, CPA) and exams required for admission to educational institutions (GRE, ACT, SAT).

Logs are abbreviated lists of observations made, tasks finished, or readings completed. The evaluator can quantitatively and perhaps objectively evaluate student work through logs. But because little reflection or writing is utilized, logs should not be the only means to evaluate students' processes and completed products. Timed writing logs in a keyboarding classroom quantify how many timings are completed in a given time period. Diverse students may need adjustments on the number of items required in their logs.

Portfolios. A portfolio is an authenticated real-world evaluation tool. Occupations such as architecture, graphic arts, and journalism rely upon professional portfolios to showcase the applicant's skills and knowledge. Through the work samples and artifacts in the portfolio, prospective employers can readily see proof of talent, knowledge, and skills.

Portfolios in a learning environment can produce the same evaluation results but also include student reflection on what was learned, what was experienced, and how the individual grew or changed with the process. While the products or artifacts in a portfolio are important, they share equal importance with the reflective pieces of the learner.

Learning experiences that can be assessed well with portfolios include skill development in such courses as keyboarding, word processing, and desktop publishing. A longitudinal look at the learner's progress toward a career goal is also well represented in a portfolio. Portfolios may be used in the job application process and may be a graduation requirement.

Teacher preparation institutions are now requiring portfolios for two major reasons. Not only is the portfolio useful to teacher candidates in the job application process, accrediting agencies and state education agencies are requiring portfolios for teacher education program evaluation. State and/or national teaching standards are used as common criteria for assessing teacher education programs.

Northwest Missouri State University, for example, is following the Missouri Department of Elementary and Secondary Education's requirement of portfolios for their teacher candidates (*Professional Portfolio Development*, 1998). An electronic template listing the 10 state standards and suggested items to use as evidence are outlined for students. This portfolio is designed to be used for teacher education program evaluation but will also be useful for curriculum improvement.

The National Board for Professional Teaching Standards (2000) uses portfolios to evaluate teacher effectiveness. Portfolios and testing at assessment centers are the means by which the teaching professional is assessed.

Universities and colleges also require portfolios of faculty in the promotion and tenure process. Portfolios document the faculty member's activities in categories such as teaching, service, student support, and research and creative activities and serve as the means to assess teacher effectiveness.

The basic elements of a portfolio remain the same whether produced traditionally on paper or electronically. Self-reflection, collection, and selection are still present, but technological skills can be better illustrated if portfolios are produced electronically. Electronic portfolios that are Web-based or stored magnetically are often utilized. However, paper portfolios may remain the preference of interviewers and employers for some time until electronic platforms are more universal and reviewers more comfortable with various technologies used to view electronic portfolios.

All students are on the "same level" when called on to prepare a portfolio. Portfolios are more personal than are other assessment tools and allow for creativity, individuality, and reflection. Diverse learners may need guidance in beginning the portfolio and organizing it, but the contents are meant to be original and unique—a benefit to all learners.

Development of Assessment Instruments

In order to be effective, assessment strategies must be both valid and reliable. Valid strategies measure what was intended to be measured. Reliability ensures consistency both by multiple evaluators and by repeated assessment episodes.

Checklists and scoring guides (rubrics) can be highly valid if descriptors are used to identify the required skills or affective traits. Two descriptors that could be used to evaluate a student's voice during an oral presentation are correct pronunciation in speech and volume appropriate for all in the room to hear.

Reliable instruments share the same questions, descriptors, or criteria for all learners to meet. The criteria are clear, identifiable, and measurable. Reliability may be increased if multiple evaluators are trained in the use of the prescribed assessment instrument. When multiple evaluators use the instrument, they should score the learning activity within a similar range of scores.

Checklists. In developing a checklist, criteria to be met or applied in completing the assignment are listed, giving students clear direction for successful completion of the learning activity. This advance knowledge of expected traits or behaviors is especially helpful to diverse students. The evaluator checks or marks the presence or absence of a specified trait or behavior. Room for comments is usually provided. Activities in the business classroom suitable for evaluation by a checklist are oral presentations, the formatting of business documents, and keyboarding technique.

Scoring guides. While a checklist simply lists the criteria, a scoring guide (rubric) describes the criteria at various performance levels. For example, if four grade levels are sought (A, B, C, D), the expected traits or behaviors are described using demonstrative verbs that clearly define and differentiate among the four levels. Three or four levels are advised. More levels would make it difficult to delineate each level. With only two levels, not enough difference would exist.

Suggestions for writing rubrics include

1. Determine how many levels of performance need to be defined.
2. Write the standard—the level all students should be able to achieve—for the performance, product, or understanding first.
3. Begin to brainstorm knowledge, skills, and qualities that would be exhibited by a person who has attained the proficiency.
4. When possible, focus on presence of behaviors rather than absence of behaviors; avoid negatives.
5. When possible, avoid relying on adverbs and adjectives to define the distinctions among levels of performance. Try to identify clear distinctions in behavior.
6. Use the first draft over a period of time as students are observed in the classroom. Continue to revise rubrics until they provide an accurate description (Mid-continent Regional Educational Library Institute, 1995).

Two types of scoring guides are analytic and holistic. Analytic scoring guides assess separate components of the task or product, usually awarding a score per criteria. The sum of all criteria constitutes the final score. Analytic scoring guides are more clearly presented in a table or chart. Holistic scoring guides give one overall rating that is based on the compilation of all criteria. They are written in a narrative or paragraph form (Edwards, 1992).

Learner input in the development of assessment instruments is important. Involvement in the development gives the learner ownership in the learning activity. Criteria by which students will be evaluated should be clear in their minds from this process. Learners can also be asked to give an assessment instrument a "dry run" to test the accuracy and effectiveness of the instrument.

Alternative Delivery of Traditional Assessment

Not only is assessment available in different formats today, but it is also being alternatively delivered to students via online methods. Two online methods are viable: computerized testing in a school-based laboratory or testing center and online testing via the Word Wide Web.

Placement and high stakes assessments, such as the GRE, GMAT, and credentialing examinations, are computerized and administered directly to individuals at testing centers (Greenburg, 1998). At schools and colleges, teachers are utilizing online testing packages for the administration of formative and summative evaluations in courses. Online test questions can be used for review and study by students and then implemented as an examination.

Web-based courses find the learner and teacher separated by distance; therefore, Web-delivered testing is used. Web course editors, such as *CourseInfo* (Blackboard Inc., 1999), often include a testing component that delivers traditional assessment electronically. Objective questions, such as multiple choice and true/false, can be generated from an assessment pool of questions and randomized. The tests can be timed and automatically scored. The scores are then placed directly in the electronic gradebook.

Other online testing tools are available for the teacher. Results can be scored and then delivered to one's e-mail address or simply submitted for evaluation by the instructor. Exam Creation Tool (http://www.igb.umontreal.ca/~leon/exam.html) and Ed Tech Tools (http://www.motted.hawaii.edu/) are two examples of online testing tools.

Security, honesty among learners, and learner identification are other concerns that have evolved from the use of online testing. Security of the test items is a concern to teachers delivering the examination via the Web. It is possible for students to complete "screen dumps" of the test questions, print the test, and share test questions in any way with peers. One way to circumvent these possibilities is to have a pool of questions from which randomized tests are made, ensuring that the 15 questions one student receives are very different from the 15 questions another student receives.

Testing packages have many options and can be set up so that the exam can only be attempted once. If the student wants to exit out and try again, access would be denied, and the exam score would be low or a zero.

When testing is unmonitored, how does one know that "Johnny" is actually taking the test and not "Billy"? One doesn't. Veteran teachers of online testing indicate that honesty and integrity among students must be a given. One must just assume Johnny is taking the test for himself. Educators should not rely on examinations as the sole means of assessment in Web-based classes, however. They should employ several other assessment measures to monitor student progress and achievement (*Online Testing*, 1999).

Berger and Garcia (1999) identified criteria to use in selecting online testing packages. The criteria include types of questions available, use of graphics/multimedia, types of feedback to students, ways questions are handled, issues of security, and means to report and track tests.

Advantages of online testing. Both teachers and learners benefit from online testing. Learners receive instant feedback on their results. Often the feedback is specific as to what section or pages of a textbook should be reviewed. Teachers often allow the learners to take practice exams not only to become comfortable with the system but also to utilize the available questions as review or exam preparation. Teachers report that speed in scoring the exams as well as flexible times at which exams can be offered are major advantages. Exams can be taken by students outside of class time at another site or via the Web. Therefore, class time is more efficiently used for instruction rather than testing.

Disadvantages of online testing. Learners indicate that online testing may or may not match their learning styles, especially if they are kinesthetic or hands-on learners. ESL learners and other diverse learners may find the reading of questions from a computer monitor difficult and more time consuming. Having timed tests may not be advantageous to these students. Depending on the package, individuals may or may not be able to return to answered questions to change their responses. Many students are apprehensive that their results will not be received or that the system will fail during the testing period. The nontechnologically oriented student can also be at a disadvantage.

Objective test questions and those with definitive answers work best with online testing. However, such questions often measure only lower-level cognitive learning; higher-level cognitive knowledge is thought by many to be best measured by observations, written assignments, and essay questions. Written assignments and essay questions can be delivered and received via online means, but observations have yet to be refined. Another disadvantage is the possibility of computer failure or inaccessibility via the network or Web. A testing backup procedure needs to be in place. Finally, online testing programs can be administratively time consuming to set up because of the need to input a pool of questions.

Assessment in the Future

As more learning is delivered via distance education, online testing will be refined and made more secure. Learner identity and security will be verified by retinal scans, voice prints, and fingerprints, and ongoing handwriting analysis during the test (Tulloch and Thompson, 1999).

Alternative assessment strategies and delivery methods effectively meet the needs of learners and allow for assessment of what all business students should know and be able to accomplish. Students do not learn in the same way; therefore, one type of assessment may not best assess all learners. With the demographic changes in our nation, learners will be more and more diverse in the future. Multiple assessment measures will be necessary to best monitor their progress and achievement.

Alternative assessment measures will also be utilized by organizations and accreditation agencies to evaluate programs and review curricula. Teacher evaluations by administration and certification agencies, too, will utilize varied assessment measures to promote, reward, and certify teachers. Portfolios will continue to be valuable assessment measures among professionals. The National Board for Professional Teaching Standards is gaining more applicants each year and is certifying more teachers through this method.

Other certifications (MOUS, MCSE, A+, CISCO) will gain prominence among professionals, especially in the computer field. High-tech, highly-skilled workers will become certified through industry-standard assessments to "show proof of what they know" and for promotion and personal growth.

Summary

When varied assessment strategies are used—process, written, and portfolios—multiple dimensions of the learner are identified. Process assessment allows one to see the manner in which the learner completed the task. Written assessments are valid means to measure higher-level cognitive skills and knowledge. Portfolios include artifacts the learner has selected to demonstrate skills. Self-reflection within a portfolio allows for the student to discuss what was learned, what was experienced, and how the individual grew or changed.

Business educators should utilize multiple assessment measures, both traditional and alternative, to best evaluate the learner's progress and achievement. Evaluation can still be accomplished via paper and pencil, but new delivery systems and methods will enhance the creation, administration, and scoring of assessment measures.

References

Berger, R., & Garcia, J. (1999, December 2). *Overview of criteria for evaluating testing software* [Online]. Available: http://www.mdcc.edu.ctd/testing

Blackboard Inc. (1999, May 19). *CourseInfo* [Online]. Available: http://www.blackboard.net/

Department of Curriculum and Instruction. (1998). *Professional portfolio development.* Maryville, MO: Northwest Missouri State University.

Edwards, L. (1992). *Developing outcome aligned assessments.* Lawrence, KS: Academic Management Systems, Inc.

Greenburg, R. (1998, March). Online testing. *Techniques,* 73, 26–28.

McEwen, B., & McEwen, T. (1996). Diversity in the classroom. In H. Perreault (Ed.), *Classroom strategies: The methodology of business education, 1996 NBEA Yearbook* (No. 34, pp. 74–86). Reston, VA: National Business Education Association.

Mid-continent Regional Educational Library (McREL) Institute. (1995). *Guidelines for writing rubrics.* Unpublished Workshop Material. Aurora, CO: McREL Institute. Used by permission of McREL.

National Board for Professional Teaching Standards. (2000, January 15). [Online]. Available: http://www.nbpts.org

National Business Education Association. (1995). *National standards for business education: What America's students should know and be able to do in business.* Reston, VA: National Business Education Association.

Online testing: Assessment and evaluation of distance learners [Teleconference]. (1999, December 2). PBS Adult Learning Satellite Service.

Ownby, A., & Perreault, H. (1994). Teaching students to understand and value diversity. *Business education forum, 48,* 27–29.

Tulloch, J., & Thompson, S. (1999, Spring/Summer). Identity, security, and testing issues in distance education. *AGENDA: Teaching, Technology, and Distance Learning,* 18–19.

Zeliff, N., & Schultz, K. (1998). *Authentic assessment in action: Preparing for the business workplace.* Little Rock, AR: Delta Pi Epsilon.

Rubric- and Portfolio-Based Assessment: Focusing on Student Progress

Marcia Bush
Santa Clara County Regional Occupational Program
Gilroy, California

Michael Timms
WestEd
San Francisco, California

Accountability for student performance is an issue that has affected every level of the educational system. Teachers must increasingly provide more information about student achievement for a variety of stakeholders. This demand for accountability raises questions about what kind of preparation should be used to enhance student performance and how teachers should recognize and measure effective learning.

The typical way to evaluate what students have learned is to use assessment as an end point. However, waiting until the end is often too late in terms of preparing students for the workplace or for the next educational level. The necessary search then is for ways to focus on assessing student progress or to evaluate student work along the way. In addition, it is not enough for the teacher to do the assessing. Students must also take responsibility for their learning, evaluate their progress, and set individual goals for achievement.

Two strategies that will accomplish both purposes are the use of rubrics to measure learning and the use of portfolios to provide a picture of student achievement.

Rubrics as a Way to Describe Student Progress

The use of rubrics or scoring guides has become a widely accepted basis for providing information about student progress. Standards or expectations for student performance are set, instructional strategies and activities developed, and evaluation checkpoints established. The critical information provided by a rubric answers one or more of the following questions:

- How do both pupil and teacher know that the student has acquired the knowledge?
- What aspects of the student's performance indicate progress?
- What does the student still need to work on?
- Has the student mastered the standards for this course or grade level?
- Is the student ready for the next stage of instruction?
- Can the student advance to the next educational level?
- Is the student prepared to enter the workforce?

What is a rubric? A rubric is defined as the title or heading, as of a chapter or a law, written or printed in red or in special lettering. Historically, red coloring was used to mark or call attention to the rules in documents. In education, the word rubric is used interchangeably with scoring guide or rating scale to designate an instrument used to provide information about "the rules" for student work.

Rubrics or scoring guides, as some prefer to call them, provide the essential connection between instruction and assessment. This connection motivates teachers to actually define the dimensions or criteria that make up the expected results before they see them. It is a critical view of the end result prior to planning instruction. When teachers see the results, the rubric enables them to clearly identify what a student has achieved.

The language of the rubric gives a word picture that describes the characteristics and level of each student's performance. In addition, the rubric "language" becomes a common denominator for discussion of student learning with colleagues within a subject area, with teachers across a campus, with community stakeholders and business partners, and with individual students or the entire class. It should also facilitate an internal discussion that enables a teacher to reflect on how students have performed and what needs to occur in order to improve performance. This view of student performance provides a connection among a fully developed set of standards; a framework for learning; a variety of engaging classroom activities; and an end-of-unit, end-of-section, and/or end-of-course examination.

Rubric-based assessment brings the process full circle. A rubric provides a format or framework for reporting performance results that is more definitive than a single numerical score or a letter grade. The information presented in a rubric ties characteristics of student performance to specific criteria or developmental stages. Further explanation of rubrics is offered by many that work in the field of assessment. According to Bailey and McTighe (1996), a scoring rubric consists of a fixed measurement scale (such as four to six points) and a set of criteria that describe the characteristics for each score point. Herman, Aschbacher, and Winters (1992) indicate that sample criteria have four common elements:

1. One or more traits or dimensions that serve as the basis for judging the student response,
2. Definitions and examples to clarify the meaning of each trait or dimension,
3. A scale of values (or a counting system) on which to rate each dimension, and
4. Standards of excellence for specified performance levels accompanied by models or examples of each level.

How Does a Rubric Work in Actual Practice?

Start with a standard and a performance expectation. The link to standards provides the answer to the question, "What should a student know and be able to do?" For example, one of the information standards outlined in the *National Standards for Business Education* is the application of information systems to organizations. The achievement standard involves a student's ability to "select and use word processing, desktop publishing, database, spreadsheet, presentation graphics, multimedia, and imaging software and industry-and subject-specific software." A performance expectation is to "use presentation and multimedia software to design, create, import data/graphics/scanned images/sound/video, and edit, format, sequence, and produce a variety of presentations."

Students in an information systems course or program at the secondary or postsecondary level, for example, would be expected to demonstrate their achievement of the knowledge and skills connected with this standard by producing several presentations.

Identify the dimensions as a basis for judging the performance.
Possible dimensions of or criteria for the information systems presentation mentioned above could be software selection and usage, design criteria, and presentation format, sequence, and delivery. The beginning development of the rubric might look something like Table 1.

Table 1
Dimensions
Software selection
Use of software
Design criteria
Presentation format
Presentation sequence
Presentation delivery

Provide a definition for the dimensions.
The next step would be to define or give characteristics for each dimension of the expected performance to be considered as achieving the standard.
In developing the scoring dimensions, Herman, Aschbacher, and Winters (1992) advise asking the following questions:

- What are the attributes of a good performance?
- By what qualities or features can excellent performance be recognized?
- What should teachers expect to see if the task is done excellently, acceptably, or poorly?
- Are there samples or models of student work to exemplify the criteria?

In Table 2, the definitions or characteristics are added to the dimensions originally shown in Table 1.

Table 2

Software selection	The software selected is appropriate for the purpose of the presentation.
Use of software	Data, graphics, and images are imported and combined to enhance the message being delivered.
Design criteria	The principles of good design are demonstrated.
Presentation format	Print, graphics, and multimedia are brought together in a coherent presentation.
Presentation sequence	Consideration of audience is evident in how the presentation is sequenced.
Presentation delivery	A clear message with introduction, objectives, content, and conclusion is delivered.

Set a scale or rating system. Further development of the rubric would involve the determination of a scale, rating system, or a way to value or judge performance. The rubric should always be written and arranged in a way that the student can understand. The value or levels can be identified in words or numbers (sometimes called cut points). Some examples of words or labels included are detailed in Table 3.

Table 3

Advanced	Exceptional Work	Goes Beyond	You Get It
Proficient	Quality Work	Fully Achieves	You Almost Get It
Basic	In Progress	Adequately Achieves	You Will Get It in the Future
	Needs Rethinking	Limited Achievement	Back to the Drawing Board

Adapted from *Community Outreach: Focusing on Assessment*, 1997.

To illustrate the next steps, two dimensions are taken from Table 2. In Table 4, the rating scale chosen is advanced, proficient, basic. Next, descriptors of performance for each dimension are developed to provide further definition of performance levels. The added definition spells out what students should be demonstrating and identifies performance expectations.

In reality, detailed definitions would then be developed for all dimensions of the rubric and all levels of performance. Defining the dimensions for each rating is the critical thinking that must be done by each teacher to communicate performance standards.

Table 4

Dimensions	Advanced	Proficient	Basic
Use of software	Data, graphics, and images are skillfully imported and combined to enhance the message being delivered.	Data, graphics, and images are imported and combined to enhance the message being delivered.	Data, graphics, and images are imported and combined but do not enhance the message being delivered.
Presentation delivery	A very logical, seamless message includes introduction, objectives, content, and conclusion.	A clear message with introduction, objectives, content, and conclusion is delivered.	The message delivered may be missing some essential components and/or delivered in such a way that they are not clearly recognizable.

Developing the Practice of Using Rubrics

The use of rubrics is a promising practice that can improve teaching and learning. However, the emphasis is on the word "practice" because there is no off-the-shelf or one-size-fits-all rubric. The development of a rubric or rubrics for use in a variety of classroom situations does take time.

Listed below are some guidelines or suggestions that will show how the practice might work more effectively and efficiently.

Continually improve the rubric. Expect to revise the descriptors of performance each time the rubric is used. Various unanticipated factors will become apparent through actual use. For instance, the examination of student work may show that there is not enough differentiation of performance for a four-point scale and that one with three points will work better.

Collect student work. Spend time identifying two types of student work. First of all, there will be the work that is a perfect example of a proficient or advanced performance in every dimension. This is the collection that becomes the benchmarks of expected performance. In contrast, there will be examples that do not line up so perfectly. This will require judgment about the individual dimensions related to the overall rating. The answer to the question about how many dimensions must fall within a given rating number or category in order for the work to receive that overall rating will depend upon what is valued.

The decision could be made that in order to receive a proficient or advanced evaluation, a student must not receive a basic rating on any dimension of the performance. In other cases, an advanced rating on one dimension could be averaged with a basic rating on another dimension to receive an overall proficient rating. Here, too, a collection of the work will help to provide valuable information about actual student performance.

Work with students to build capacity. Provide rubrics for students earlier rather than later. According to Grant Wiggins (1993) all successful performers know their target and standards, not just their task. Teachers should keep a range of examples of student work to use in a variety of ways. These examples can be used as models giving students an opportunity to actually see what a proficient or advanced paper or performance looks like. Students can use an unmarked set of papers or projects to practice with the rating scale or rubric. This hands-on practice for students may be one of the most effective ways to provide coaching about expected performance based on a rubric.

Finally, after having some experience with the use of rubrics to evaluate their work, students could be given the responsibility of developing a rubric. In all cases, the student's understanding of the relationship between what is expected and what is produced becomes much clearer.

What Are the Advantages of Using Rubrics or Scoring Guides?

Accurate communication about the criteria for successful performance. Many would agree that the operative word is communication (ASCD Yearbook, 1996) or feedback (Marzano, 1998, Schmoker, 1996). The definitions of performance provided by the rubric become the basis for conversations about student work. The most important participant in that conversation is the student. According to Marzano, the primary purpose of grading is to provide feedback that is as accurate and precise as possible so that students can improve their achievement. Through the use of a rubric or scoring guide, the response provided is immediate and relevant.

Increased objectivity and reliability in the assessment process. The investment of time to look at the expected end result that will demonstrate knowledge, skills, and ability, and define both the characteristics and levels of possible performance puts the teacher, assessor, or evaluator in a much more neutral position. This focus on the end result enables a teacher to be free of the influence of other important but not directly related variables (such as the fact that the student has good attendance or a good attitude, always completes assignments on time, etc.). In the absence of confounding variables, a teacher is more able to provide a consistent, comparable rating across an entire set of student papers or projects.

For an assessment to be reliable, the following requirements must be met:

1. Several evaluators must look at the same task or work sample and reach the same conclusion about the quality of the work;

2. The same individual must reach the same conclusion when looking at student work a second time; and

3. The student performance must remain at a consistent level on different performance occasions because the performance expectation is clearly understood.

Increased student engagement due to understanding of how to improve performance. Clear guidelines contribute to a new learning atmosphere or community where students are learning what they can do and how they can improve. The students are able to discuss their work in terms of its quality.

Types of Rubrics

Analytic. An analytic rubric breaks a single performance or a compilation of performances into separate parts, and provides a rating point for each portion. A final total is a sum of the parts, each weighted separately and then collectively. This disaggregation of performance data may be more likely to provide specific feedback to improve learning (Herman, Aschbacher, and Winters, 1992). Separate ratings can be provided for different aspects of an assigned task. This type of rubric is most often used as learning progresses or as a formative evaluation. Referring to the example of the information systems presentation in Table 2, a student might have been evaluated on individual pieces of work that were completed leading up to the final presentation.

Holistic. In contrast, a holistic rubric focuses on an entire performance or event as a single dimension. A single score represents overall quality directly related to a criterion. This type of rubric is used at the end point such as the end of a unit, section, or course as a summative assessment. A rubric used for portfolio assessment would be an example. The individual pieces of the portfolio may have been evaluated separately outside of the portfolio. Then, a holistic view is taken when all the pieces are combined and a single rating on the overall quality is provided.

Rubrics and the Relationship to Scores or Grades

A checklist is really a simplified rubric used to check off the presence or absence of characteristics or behaviors. However, a checklist does not provide information about the quality of the characteristic in performance terms. Moving from using a checklist to using a detailed rubric, in which characteristics of performance are aligned with a rating scale, means being able to provide more specific information about what the student has accomplished.

Many checklists or cover sheets typically used in business education courses can provide the dimensions for a rubric. An example of a checklist for the information systems presentation might look like the example shown in Table 5.

Table 5	
	Points
Software selected (5 points)	_____
Use of software (10 points)	_____
Design criteria demonstrated (15 points)	_____

In the example above, the points will vary depending on what decisions are being made. Notice that the numerical scale represents a range, but there is no stated or agreed upon way to determine how to assign a value within the range.

Uses of Rubrics

Although the focus of this discussion of rubric-based assessment has been primarily on uses applied to business education classroom settings, it is not hard to imagine a much wider use. In fact, the possibilities are limitless. In all cases, the rubric provides the essential definition and focus for the assessment of performance. Several possibilities include use across the curriculum, use for self-evaluation or peer evaluation, and even use from a wider stakeholder perspective.

Across the curriculum or across a program. The same writing rubric could be used by teachers from many disciplines or of several different courses within a discipline. The teachers in this case would be coming together to examine student work with a common goal. For example, this goal might be improvement of writing. A simplified rubric might have dimensions or criteria for organization, supporting details, and mechanics as shown in Table 6.

Using this rubric, teachers from various disciplines or courses could gather to share and discuss student work. The intent of the discussion would be to compare how students perform across several courses. The end result of this effort could be the establishment of benchmarks for all courses or disciplines that are communicated to students in a more global way and reinforced through individual course standards. Examination of student work in this way has the potential to improve the quality of writing on a schoolwide, districtwide, or systemwide basis.

Self-evaluation or peer evaluation. Students, too, can become involved with the use of rubrics. Continuing with the example above, one can see that students can refer to the rubric as they are writing. Cooperative groups can be coached in the process of peer review. The role of the teacher in both cases is as a facilitator to help build student skill in using the process.

Wider stakeholder perspective. The ultimate and perhaps most powerful use of rubrics occurs when the wider community is invited to take part in the

---

Table 6

4   Fully accomplishes ...
- Effective organization, logical paragraphs, and clear transition sentences are established between each new supporting thought.
- Supporting details, examples, and facts are meaningful.
- Mechanics (spelling, punctuation, usage) are flawless.

3   Substantially accomplishes ...
- Clear organization; paragraphs are developed and presented so that the point of the message is understood.
- Supporting details, examples, and facts add interest.
- Mechanics are almost flawless; there are no run-on sentences or sentence fragments.

2   Partially accomplishes ...
- Organization is somewhat difficult to follow.
- Supporting details, examples, and facts leave the reader asking questions and wanting more information.
- Mechanics are becoming a problem; there are some run-on sentences and/or sentence fragments.

1   Little or no progress ...
- Organization needs developing; transitional words are almost nonexistent or, if present, are repeated.
- Supporting details need developing.
- Mechanics are in the way; paper is extremely difficult to read.

Adapted from *Community Outreach: Focusing on Assessment*, 1997.

---

assessment or evaluation of student work. A well-articulated, publicly visible rubric can become the meeting ground that facilitates a shared understanding of what the student should know and be able to do.

With the use of rubrics established as a sound practice, attention turns to the actual work students would be producing. The portfolio is a major performance piece that uses a rubric.

Portfolios as a Picture of Student Progress

Artists and designers have used portfolios for many years to show collections of the work that demonstrates their skills and creativity. In recent years, a tremendous surge of interest has occurred in the use of portfolios in both education and the business world. In education, portfolios are being used as a flexible way of assessing students' skills and abilities in realistic ways. In business, it is increasingly common for professionals to keep portfolios that illustrate their accomplishments in their field for use in job interviews. Business education is in an ideal position to blend these two purposes.

Where Do Portfolios Fit?

The most common use of assessments in education is to measure student progress as a way of promoting learning. Portfolios offer the chance to monitor student growth over a period of time (Herman, Aschbacher, and Winters, 1992) and can be a powerful stimulant in the learning process. Of particular interest to business educators is the fact that portfolios can be designed to assess work-based knowledge and skills.

What Are the Advantages of Using Portfolios for Assessment?

Flexibility. A portfolio is really a shell or framework into which student work can be slotted. For a portfolio to work well, there should be a set of guidelines that define for the students what is (and is not) to be included in the portfolio. This will help clarify what is expected of the students. For example, in a business communications course, the portfolio guidelines might require the student to include an example of a document produced using desktop publishing software that is also a writing sample showing communication skills.

On the other hand, portfolio guidelines for students in a marketing course might require them to develop a marketing plan for a new local business and to create a customer database using appropriate software. Portfolios can include whatever is appropriate to the course or set of business education standards. However, a balance needs to be struck between giving students a framework that guarantees they will demonstrate appropriate knowledge and skills, and allowing them some freedom to choose what to include.

Student interest. Giving students choices in what work they complete and select for their portfolios is a powerful way to motivate them. Programs using alternative assessments like portfolios report increased levels of student motivation and interest (California Assessment Collaborative, 1993; McLaughlin and Hipps, 1997). Students also begin to take increasing responsibility for their learning.

Portfolios provide opportunities for students to evaluate their own work. When rubrics are shared with students from the start, they know what the goals are and are more likely to be able to demonstrate the knowledge and skills they possess. When given the chance to reflect on their progress, they will become empowered in the learning process. Opportunities to revise and improve work destined for the portfolio provide valuable chances to learn as students address mistakes, misunderstandings, and gaps in knowledge.

Work with real issues. Students often have difficulty seeing what relevance the subjects they are learning at school have to their life outside school or their futures. Portfolios that incorporate work that is based on real-world issues or in real-world settings (like work placements) can overcome this disconnection. For example, students may investigate the use of spreadsheets in several local businesses and report their findings.

Real tasks. In business education, teachers are often interested in how well a student is able to combine knowledge and skills learned throughout the course and apply them in an integrated way to complex tasks they will encounter in the business world. Traditional paper-and-pencil assessments often treat knowledge and skills separately, but portfolios do not suffer the same limitations. Scoring rubrics can be developed to assess different aspects of a complex performance, so that a detailed evaluation of a student's ability can be made. For example, a student who submits a work sample of an accounting balance sheet for a student-run school enterprise might be showing understanding of accounting principles, ability to use accounting software, and written communication skills.

Alignment with the curriculum. Alignment with the curriculum is essential for a meaningful portfolio. Teachers and students will invest considerable time in defining and creating work for the portfolio, so it is wasteful if it is not aligned with what students are learning in class. The portfolio is a chance for teachers to reaffirm that students are learning and for students to reflect on what they have learned. Schools that are operating career-based academies are using portfolios because they align well with an integrated curriculum in which students are blending skills from different disciplines.

North Monterey County High School in Castroville, California, for example, has students complete a project on immigration in their junior year. This involves social studies in investigating the content, English in communicating through writing, and business skills in making a computer presentation of the project to an audience.

Teachers in such schools have also discovered that working together means that one teacher does not have to be responsible for everything in a portfolio project. Students may complete different parts of the portfolio in different discipline areas, such as a writing sample in English classes; they may also complete work samples that show integrated skills. Both types of portfolio entries can exist in the same portfolio.

When an integrated portfolio is to be created, the team of teachers must spend time planning which portfolio entries are to be completed in which classes. In integrated settings, mechanisms should be developed to monitor student progress in the completion of the portfolio. Ideally, work that contributes to the portfolio is being produced throughout the period of the business education courses, so that there is not a frantic rush at the end of instruction to assemble a portfolio.

Key Features of Effective Portfolios

O'Neill and Stansbury (1999) identify key features that are shared by effective portfolio assessments. These portfolios

- Include student work reflecting multiple standards,
- Grow out of the regular classroom curriculum and students' work-based experiences, and
- Can be used to document performance improvement over time and/or to showcase overall achievement.

Formative and summative portfolio assessment. Portfolios used to document student learning and performance improvement over time are called formative working portfolios. In formative portfolios, students keep drafts of work at different stages so that both the teacher and the students can assess and reflect upon progress and learning.

Alternatively, a portfolio used to showcase overall achievement following a program or course of study is called a summative presentation portfolio (O'Neill and Stansbury, 1999). In a summative portfolio, students present work that shows evidence of overall achievement relative to a standard or learning goal. Summative portfolios might be shown to employers or college admissions officers as evidence of achievement, and in vocational education they are often called professional, career, or workplace readiness portfolios (Meggison, 1996; Troper and Smith, 1997).

A portfolio can also be both a formative and summative assessment. Formative working portfolios can readily be transformed into summative presentation portfolios. As the program of study draws to a close, students choose their best samples of work to place in the final presentation portfolio.

The Career-Technical Assessment Program (C-TAP) portfolio is an example of a portfolio designed to help students in career-technical programs, like business, to prepare for postsecondary training and work by: (1) requiring demonstration of knowledge and skills in the workplace; (2) showcasing students' best work to potential employers, colleges, and training programs; and (3) improving students' ability to plan work, document progress, identify strengths and weaknesses in their work, and refine and improve their work over time. The structure of the C-TAP portfolio is shown in Table 7.

Work samples—the heart of a solid portfolio. Of the teachers using portfolios for a variety of purposes, it seems that teachers who already use project-based learning and other extended learning tasks are the most ready to use portfolios as an assessment tool. Teachers working on career portfolios in Modesto, California, found that, as a rule of thumb, work samples of suitable depth for inclusion in a portfolio took between two to five class periods for a student to complete, depending on the complexity of the task.

Work samples for a business education portfolio can take many forms. Robert Hughes, a business teacher at Orange Glen High School in Escondido,

---

Table 7

Introduction ("Portfolio Presentation")
Table of contents
Letter of introduction

Career Development Package
Résumé
Employment or college application
Letter of recommendation

Work Samples
Four examples and descriptions of work, demonstrating mastery of important career-technical standards

Writing Sample
A sample of writing, demonstrating investigative, analytical, and writing abilities

Supervised Practical Experience Evaluation (Optional)
Documentation of a student's practical or work experience, demonstrating workplace readiness

From *Career-Technical Assessment Program: 1999 Student Guidebook.* WestEd (1999).

California, explains the projects he does with his marketing and entrepreneurship classes:

> There is flexibility in the selection of work samples. Most frequently, the work samples include sections of a business plan, which include business descriptions, financial reports, selection of locations, marketing ideas, personnel policies, store layouts, and other factors in a business plan. Many students have designed products to market, and they develop their ideas around this concept. Last year, a student designed a Boogie Board with a place to put keys so they didn't have to be left on the beach. He included drawings, cost analysis, advertising, and even a prototype in his final portfolio. The final writing sample was a complete business plan that could be presented to a banker [when] requesting financial backing.

Examples of work samples suitable for a business education portfolio are shown in Table 8.

Some work sample products are easy to incorporate into a portfolio binder, such as the newsletter example; but others, like the Web page example, do not lend themselves to presentation on paper. Creating an electronic portfolio, in which all the components are saved electronically, can allow items like a Web page or a database to be displayed to the viewer. A sales presentation, for instance, can be videotaped, and the tape can become part of the portfolio. Photographs, drawings, or diagrams can be used to show such work as a product display.

Table 8	
Business communications	Design and creation of a newsletter for a school organization
	A sales presentation to a potential customer
Marketing	Market research report and database of information gathered about various companies
Business technology	Creation of a Web page advertising a new product
Finance	A report on investment options for a cash lump sum

Ideally, by the end of the year, students will have completed several projects that have generated work relevant to the goals of the portfolio so that they can select the work samples that best illustrate their range of skills and knowledge. To make this possible, it is important to have students work on such projects early on and to continue with different assignments throughout the year. Assignments should be closely linked to the goals of the portfolio and designed to illustrate the particular skills or standards that are the focus of instruction.

Summaries—a key to understanding. No matter which items are included in a portfolio, a short written summary that explains each work sample can add illuminating details. Portfolios have been described as offering a "window into the students' minds, a means for both staff and students to understand the educational process at the level of the individual learner" (Paulson, Paulson, and Meyer, 1991).

Writing the summaries is also a metacognitive process for the students in which they must reflect upon what they have learned in order to explain what their work samples show and how they illustrate their newfound knowledge and skills. If the portfolio is based on standards or skills, the work sample summary is where students can describe which standards are demonstrated in their work.

For the reader, the summary provides an insight into the thinking and decisions behind the work sample. It may show the student's depth of knowledge, which is not always obvious when looking at only the work sample. For example, a printout from a market research database might be accompanied by a summary explaining how the data for the database was gathered, why the information is important for researching the market, and how the database could help a company wanting to launch a product in that market.

Other portfolio entries. If the portfolio is intended for use beyond the classroom, there are some portfolio entries that will add to its usefulness for the student. A common portfolio entry is a résumé because this is a helpful summary of the student's achievements for prospective employers or college admissions officers. For example, at the Francis Drake High School in San Anselmo, California, completing the résumé provided students with some unanticipated benefits.

The process of reflecting upon what to put into the résumé made students address issues about their future goals. It also gave students confidence as they articulated what they had done well.

Peoria High School in Peoria, Arizona, chose to have students complete a "student information sheet" in which they recorded all the information they needed for filling out employment or college applications. The sheet helped students to reflect about their achievements and to be prepared by having the sheet handy when asked in an application for the names, addresses, and telephone numbers of two people who could provide references.

Another type of portfolio entry linked to the résumé is a letter of reference from an adult who knows the student and his or her achievements. The adult may be the teacher, but a portfolio is strengthened when others like supervisors at work or community leaders provide references.

Another entry that fronts many portfolios intended for use outside of school is a personal statement by the student. This introduces the student to the reader of the portfolio and demonstrates his or her ability to communicate; to organize ideas; and to reflect on his or her skills, achievements, and goals.

In business education, teachers are often interested in enhancing students' written and oral communication skills. Portfolio entries can be designed to elicit examples of student capabilities in these areas. It is easy to require a writing sample as part of the portfolio, and the topic may be narrowly or widely defined. An example of a business education topic is "Marketing to Multicultural Buyers," which could include a description of how marketing strategies are changing to meet the needs of multicultural consumers, and an assessment of the impact of these new marketing strategies on profits.

The closer the topic is to the curricular goals of the class, the better picture the teacher will obtain of the students' knowledge in business education, in addition to assessing their writing skills. There are also different types of writing, and the instructor may want to assign a project based around persuasive writing related to selling and advertising, rather than informational writing on a business topic.

Assessing oral communication is not as straightforward as assessing written communication. The C-TAP student project at WestEd in San Francisco, California, includes an oral presentation in which students are required to prepare, practice, and deliver a three-minute presentation of a project they have prepared. When used as part of a portfolio, the presentation can become an extension of the work sample, keeping a tight linkage across the portfolio.

It is possible to assess other types of oral communication, such as a sales presentation to a customer, instead of an informational presentation. Incorporating the oral presentation into the portfolio can be achieved by use of a video camera. Evaluation of the oral communication skills can be done as the presentation is being made or later by viewing the videotape. There are advantages to assessing the performance as it happens because it is easier to detect how the audience is receiving the presentation and how the speaker is reacting to the audience. If no videotaping of the presentation is possible, a copy of the evaluation of the student's presentation can be included on its own.

Portfolios can also incorporate evidence of what a student is achieving outside of the classroom. For example, evidence of work done as part of supervised job placements or documentation of relevant voluntary work, such as producing a newsletter for a local charity, can be included.

Scoring the Portfolio

The advantages of using rubrics to score complex student work have already been discussed. Rubrics are also an ideal tool for scoring student portfolios. The C-TAP developed at WestEd uses a four-step process for scoring portfolios as shown in Table 9.

Table 9

Step 1
Review the portfolio for completeness; all required sections and entries should be present in order for the portfolio to receive an overall (holistic) score.

Step 2
Carefully read and examine each of the portfolio entries.

Step 3
After reading and examining the entire portfolio, score the portfolio according to the dimensions (traits) specified in the rubric.

Step 4
Keeping in mind all the dimension scores, assign an overall (holistic) score to the portfolio, and provide a written justification for the score.

Portfolios may also be scored as each piece of work for them is produced. The advantage of doing so is that students get early feedback on the quality of their work and can be given the chance to revise and refine work that will eventually become part of the portfolio. The process of revision is a learning experience in itself.

Summary

Developing rubric and portfolio assessment methods is hard work, especially when they are new to teachers and students. They often require a shift from teacher-led to student-led instruction, which can be unnerving for teacher and student alike. Changing a curriculum to include more long-term assignments that give students choices requires time and effort, and implementing a portfolio assessment system can take a year or two before it is running smoothly.

Rubrics and portfolio-based assessments are logical partners that make it possible to focus on student progress in a very positive way. Using them also helps to foster a focus on real-world skills and practice, making rubrics and portfolio-based assessment ideal for use in business education.

References

Bailey, J., & McTighe, J. (1996). Reporting achievement at the secondary level: What and how. In Guskey, T. R. (Ed.), *ASCD Yearbook: Communicating student learning* (pp. 119–140). Alexandria, VA: Association for Supervision and Curriculum Development.

California Assessment Collaborative. (1993, September). Charting the course toward instructionally sound assessment (A Report of the Alternative Assessment Pilot Project). San Francisco: California Assessment Collaborative.

Community outreach: Focusing on assessment. (1997). Orange County Department of Education.

Guskey, T. R. (Ed.). (1996). *ASCD Yearbook: Communicating student learning.* Alexandria, VA: Association for Supervision and Curriculum Development.

Herman, J. L., Aschbacher, P. R., & Winters, L. (1992). *A practical guide to alternative assessment.* Alexandria, VA: Association for Supervision and Curriculum Development.

Marzano, R. (1998, December). Advances in grading. In *Education update.* Alexandria, VA: Association for Supervision and Curriculum Development.

McLaughlin, D., & Hipps, J. (1997). *The career preparation assessment, results and analyses from the 1996–97 pilot test: Final report.* San Francisco: WestEd.

Meggison, P. F. (1996). Programs meeting the needs of business and students. In H. R. Perreault (Ed.), *Classroom strategies: The methodology of business education, 1996 NBEA Yearbook* (No. 34, pp. 41–53). Reston, VA: National Business Education Association.

National Business Education Association. (1995). *National standards for business education: What America's students should know and be able to do in business.* Reston, VA. National Business Education Association.

O'Neill, K., & Stansbury, K. (1999). *Developing a standards-based assessment system: The ACE/C-TAP example.* San Francisco: WestEd.

Paulson, F. L., Paulson, P. R., & Meyer, A. M. (1991, February). What makes a portfolio a portfolio? *Educational Leadership, 48,* 60–63.

Schmoker, M. (1996). *Results: The key to continuous school improvement.* Alexandria, VA: Association for Supervision and Curriculum Development.

Stecher, B. M., Rahn, M. L., Ruby, A., Alt, M. N., Robyn, A., & Ward, B. (1997). *Using alternative assessments in vocational education.* Santa Monica, CA: RAND and the National Center for Research in Vocational Education at the University of California, Berkeley.

Taggart, G. L., Phifer, S. J., Nixon, J. A, & Wood, M. (Eds). (1998). *Rubrics: A handbook for construction and use.* Lancaster, PA: Technomic Publishing Co., Inc.

Troper, J., & Smith, C. (1997). Workplace readiness portfolios. In F. O'Neill, Jr. (Ed.), *Workforce readiness: Competencies and assessment.* Mahwah, NJ: Lawrence Erlbaum Associates and National Center for Research on Evaluation, Standards, and Student Testing (CRESST).

WestEd. (1999). *Career-technical assessment program: 1999 student guide-book.* San Francisco: WestEd.

WestEd. (1999). *Career-technical assessment program: 1999 teacher guide-book.* San Francisco: WestEd.

Wiggins, G. (1993). *Assessing student performance: Exploring the purpose and limits of testing.* San Francisco: Jossey-Bass Inc., Publishers.

Wiggins, G., & McTighe, J. (1998). *Understanding by design.* Alexandria, VA: Association for Supervision and Curriculum Development.

Zeliff, N. D., & Schultz, K. A. (1996). Authentic assessment. In H. R. Perreault (Ed.), *Classroom strategies: The methodology of business education, 1996 NBEA Yearbook (*No. 34, pp. 87–105). Reston, VA: National Business Education Association.

Business and Education: A Partnership for Successful Assessment

Ann A. Cooper
Central Carolina Technical College
Sumter, South Carolina

Katherine Cliatt
State Department of Education
Columbia, South Carolina

Assessment in business education has become a significant aspect of education management in today's era of accountability. As a multifaceted avenue for addressing issues throughout education, assessment affects both program content and quality if applied in a continuous cycle of review and improvement. The involvement of business in assessment has increased significantly over the past few years with legislation at the state and national levels mandating oversight by the business community. Education leaders have also recognized that business involvement in determining the effectiveness of instruction and quality of graduates is essential to the improvement of programs.

Successful business education programs have always included the participation of the business community, and assessment can be one aspect of involvement that can extend and enrich this relationship. Such involvement leads to greater integration of business with the education community and results in businesses having more in-depth knowledge about the role and challenges of education in preparing individuals for the workforce.

Networking and collaboration build stronger programs and effect working relationships that should be the cornerstone of all business education programs. The greater the involvement of business in the assessment of programs, the greater the possibilities are for improvement of these programs. However, the involvement of business in the education environment should not be limited to assessment and can produce significant returns on the investment of time and the development of relationships through collaborative efforts that will continue to benefit all partners in the education system.

The Importance of Business Involvement

The importance of business involvement in the assessment of business education lies in the validation that it provides in areas such as (1) product satisfaction and delivery, (2) competency appropriateness, (3) economic development, and (4) legislative mandates.

The business community is the ultimate customer of education and certainly of business education. Business education must provide product satisfaction and delivery through customer satisfaction to its consumer. The purposes of education are broad, complex, and multifaceted; however, a primary focus of business education is to provide the student with appropriate workplace skills to function effectively in a chosen profession.

The goals of education are similar regardless of the profession pursued, as individuals who enter the workplace must be prepared to perform their job duties and responsibilities. Businesses that hire these individuals in the fields of health care, education, government, industry, trade, commerce, transportation, or law measure the effectiveness of the education system and the individual programs based upon the performance of those who become their employees.

The level and quality of the skills attained by the graduates of business education programs communicate the competency appropriateness of a program. The nature, complexity, level, and content of knowledge of graduates are monitored by employers. It is not only important to provide education competencies, but the *appropriate* competencies must be taught in the classroom and mastered by the graduates. Business and industry expects no less than appropriate entry-level skills of employees entering the workplace.

The standards of performance for business education are founded in the need for productivity and ultimately affect the economic development of the business community. The importance of business in the assessment of the effectiveness and appropriateness of employee preparation is underscored by the significance of positive education-business relationships and a climate conducive to continued improvement of the education and training processes. An industry-based curriculum should not be simply a reworking of traditional offerings—the curriculum must effectively draw upon the experiences of students in the kinds of jobs they are most likely to obtain (Hull, 1992). Business can provide feedback that will serve as the foundation for continued improvement.

As business education has matured through the evolution of performance-based accountability mandated by federal acts, the overall definition of quality programs has come to include, among other things, job placement and academic competency attainment (Border, 1998). Validation of the appropriate level of competencies is an integral aspect of building collaborative relationships with business and industry.

The federal act with which business educators are most familiar is the Carl D. Perkins Vocational and Applied Technology Act and its reauthored versions usually referred to as Perkins II and Perkins III. One of the goals of the original Perkins Act was to "...expand, improve, modernize, and develop quality vocational education programs in order to meet the needs of the Nation's existing and future workforce..." [Section 101 (a)].

The 1998 Perkins III Act includes a new requirement for student attainment of "...challenging state established academic, and vocational and technical skill proficiencies..." and requires more accountability for achieving important results, shifting to an emphasis on outcomes, with the methods used to attain this requirement being the responsibility of the state and local administrators.

The School-to-Work Act of 1994 made it clear that the intent of the legislative bodies that fund education is to have business involved in the development of education programs. Establishing business as a partner in determining the effectiveness of business education programs is no longer an option; it is now a requirement for many critical funding sources.

Federal and state legislation requiring the involvement of business in the assessment of education programs, as well as an increased emphasis on competency-based education, economic development, and the satisfaction of business with education, have all created a climate in which collaborative efforts can prosper. Ultimately, this should be the most significant factor in the involvement of business in education and education assessment.

Through these collaborative efforts, many benefits develop as networking leads to working relationships that aid individual students, business education programs, school systems, and eventually the quality of life in communities through an appropriately trained workforce.

Aspects of Involvement of Business

The involvement of business in the assessment process depends upon the area being evaluated: an entire program, an individual course, the readiness of graduates to enter the workforce, or the facilities and instructional technology resources. Each of these areas requires different and unique approaches to the evaluation process. The extent and duration of business involvement should be appropriately defined relative to the area being assessed. Clear definition of what needs to be reviewed and the extent of involvement are critical factors in the effective use of business in the assessment process.

Program assessment should be approached holistically to determine what a graduate of the program should be able to perform upon exiting the program and entering the workforce or continuing into a higher education system. Program assessment by business can provide an opportunity for review of the comprehensiveness of the program. In the rapidly changing technology era of business education, it is very easy for programs to become one isolated course after another that results in a program that lacks threading and cohesiveness. Business can be asked to review the total curriculum to determine appropriateness of content and delivery.

Individual course development and assessment involves evaluation of course competencies. As technology continues its speed-of-light development, business assessment of individual courses can identify the competencies necessary in a particular software or technology area. Business can save business educators valuable time and energy by quickly and succinctly identifying new workplace competencies.

Assessment of graduate readiness in the workplace is one of the most valuable areas of involvement for any business education program. This is another area of holistic evaluation. The employer is looking at the total person who enters the workplace. Business is quick to communicate the importance of the mastery of many hard and soft skills to prepare an appropriate graduate who can become a productive and contributing employee. This evaluation of the graduate can be extremely valuable to business education program development and is tied directly to the content of both the program and course development. This is the customer satisfaction factor identified as a key component of business involvement.

Business can also provide invaluable assistance in the assessment of facilities and technology resources. With the continuous upgrading of equipment, facilities, and delivery resources, the capital investment required continues to accelerate. Business and industry can identify what resources are required and where these need to be used within a program of study.

A significant by-product of this process is the increased awareness of business and industry of the needs of education in acquisition of the appropriate facilities. The networking and relationship building that result from business involvement in program assessment may result in capital investment by a business to improve the delivery of instruction. Collaboration many times results in an awareness of needs and the development of resources to meet those needs.

An example of business involvement in the delivery of instruction and preparation of employees is the Cisco Networking Academies Programs being offered at the secondary and postsecondary levels throughout the United States. The Cisco Systems Corporation, a Silicon Valley-based networking company, in partnership with schools, is preparing students for the information age. The academies are models for the application of the school-to-work concept.

Cisco has developed a specific curriculum content for the preparation of individuals to establish and maintain computer networks and has provided extensive funding for setting up the facilities to deliver this instruction. The assessment aspect of Cisco's involvement is exemplified through its certification programs to ensure competency mastery. Indications are that programs similar to Cisco's will continue to develop as the need for qualified workers increases (Cisco, 1997).

Regardless of the aspect of involvement of business in the assessment process, the emphasis should be on assessment as a multifaceted means by which a program can be measured. This overall goal must be foremost in establishing the criteria of evaluation. Furthermore, it is important to focus on assessment of business education as a composite of several different approaches and evaluation methods. No single method or area reviewed yields all the information needed to determine program effectiveness.

The more information gathered from a variety of sources, the better the resulting data will be that reveal areas of strengths and weaknesses. This has been illustrated at the state level with legislation that evaluates education systems in multiple areas of performance to yield a composite score for overall effectiveness. The State Board of Education in the state of Nebraska in its Assessment Policy (1998) states, " Since each assessment process or instrument has different strengths, no single one can adequately achieve all purposes. Therefore, multiple assessment processes are necessary to provide information for teachers, parents, and policy makers." It is important for business education to develop multiple methods of evaluating programs to ensure accurate results.

Involving Business in Assessment

Strategies for involving business in the assessment of education programs must be approached from a practical and realistic standpoint by educators. Business involvement is the key element in relevant competency development to establish national, state, and local standards for business education. The strategies to involve business in the assessment of education programs are numerous and each contributes to the development of positive working relationships that can enhance the respectability of the education community. Involvement should not be limited exclusively to assessment.

Clear identification of the purpose of business involvement is paramount to establishing an effective assessment process. Defining the goals of assessment and/or involvement is an initial step in the process. Review of the planning and strategic processes for any effective education group will reveal a well-constructed purpose and mission to any external group. Essential to the process is definition of expected levels of participation and outcomes of involvement. However, even the best-planned purpose of business' involvement in the assessment process should allow for the unexpected. Many outstanding working relationships between business and education were originally founded on small or even sometimes rather different outcomes than are eventually realized.

According to the Southern Regional Education Board publication, (Bottoms, Presson, and Johnson, 1992):

> *Partnerships with business and industry are vital. Schools making the most progress listen to business and industry and involve them actively in developing programs of study that emphasize knowledge and skills for life and work. Because business leaders know what is required, they are in a unique position to provide teachers with authentic, up-to-date learning. (p. 68)*

Involvement of business in competency development may include soliciting input on course and program content in the development of course and program competencies to formulate the total curriculum. A method of acquiring this information from business and industry leaders is the process known as DACUM (Develop a Curriculum) Occupational Analysis, in which duties and tasks are identified and associated with a particular occupation. Groups of businesspeople can be brought together for a brief period of time (usually a one-day period) to identify the relevant competencies for a particular professional position.

Competencies can be identified and then classified into areas that are appropriate to certain courses within a program of study. A related method of evaluating job tasks is the Work Keys profiling process. Work Keys is a method of identifying the tasks associated with each skill level and category for a job within a profession.

As the rapid pace of change continues to accelerate, the need for course, program, and curriculum competencies has never been more critical. Business professionals can provide specific feedback as to the content, specificity, and level of knowledge and expertise required of employees, and the focus on future trends and developments as the competencies continuously change. This type of involvement leads to a truly competency-based curriculum and can be implemented at the national, state, or local levels.

Collaborative Opportunities With Business

Managers of business education programs, regardless of the level—teacher, department chair, or administrator—must identify and capitalize upon collaborative opportunities in order to effectively involve business. Many opportunities for this collaboration exist, and evidence indicates that legislative bodies as well as the business community are desirous to participate as partners in many activities in the following areas:

Education grants. The variety and sources of grants are numerous; however, there is increasing emphasis on collaboration between business and education. This represents an opportunity not only for collaboration, but also for funding resources.

Chambers of commerce committees and activities. Most chambers of commerce have active education committees or activities; they recognize that strong and viable communities have effective education systems. Chambers many times need contact from the education system indicating what kind of participation would be beneficial.

Economic development boards. Thriving communities have strong economic development or workforce development boards. Recognizing that attracting new business and industry to any area is dependent upon a sound education system to prepare the workforce is a driving factor in encouraging these bodies to work collaboratively with education personnel.

Advisory committees. Programs are usually required to have an active advisory committee that provides recommendations for program and curriculum development. It is to the benefit of all concerned to capitalize on this requirement to gather information for the improvement of education services and programs.

Mentoring programs. Many organizations within a community have mentoring programs for students. This is an opportunity to develop relationships that involve not only education personnel and the business community but the students as well.

Return to industry for faculty. Opportunities exist in many businesses for faculty to participate in industry activities that provide them with direct insight into job requirements and responsibilities. Businesses often welcome this type of activity since the educator comes to the workplace, and the interruption from job tasks or time away from the job is minimized for the businessperson.

Student internships. Similar to mentoring activities, student internships are opportunities for students to experience the business world in a learning environment. There are also opportunities for businesspeople to provide specific assessment information on the readiness of students to enter the workplace.

Articulation coordination. Articulation coordination between secondary and postsecondary institutions is another strategy for involving business in the assessment process. Articulation in its truest sense should be competency based and free of extensive testing and evaluation. Program and standards validation by business can provide input into appropriate levels of competencies. It can also contribute to the encouragement of coordinated efforts between education parties as well as lend a perspective of objectivity to the process. Business is also provided with an opportunity to assess present competencies, recommend changes, and identify areas for growth and progress in competency development.

Each of these opportunities encourages interaction, networking, and assessment to occur between the education system and the business community. These contribute to the development of an appropriate vision and delivery of instruction to enhance the business education classroom. From one activity, several related activities can develop. This is the core reason for integrating business and education. The more communication and collaboration is realized, the greater will be the understanding of what business and education need from each other and what they can contribute to each other.

Successful examples representing what the workplace expects from the business education student have been developed through the following projects:

- The *National Standards for Business Education* (NBEA, 1995) was developed and reviewed by professionals from business education across a broad spectrum of the discipline. "The primary purposes of this document are to provide the standard by which all business education programs are measured, to define anew the parameters of the discipline of business education as it has emerged in recent years, and to provide a document which curriculum writers can use as a guide in developing superior programs in business education" (p. 8).
- The National Skill Standards Board (NSSB) coordinated the development of voluntary skill standards. Several areas related to business education were on the list to have standards developed by business: financial services, business and administrative services, wholesale/retail sales, hospitality and tourism services, public administration, and legal and protective services. Where applicable, these standards from business should be incorporated into course competencies. The full text of the standards developed through NSSB is available on the Internet at http://www.nssb.org.
- The Vocational-Technical Education Consortium of States (V-TECS) has developed standards projects that incorporate tasks actually performed in three business areas: (1) administrative support occupations, 1996; (2) business financial occupations, 1998; and (3) business management occupations, 1998. Information about obtaining these three documents can be found on the Internet at http://www.mindspring.corp/~vtecs.

The Future of Assessment in Business Education

Assessment of education, and specifically business education, by the business community will continue to increase whether driven by legislation, citizens insisting on accountability, or the customer base of the education community—prospective students or the business world. Each of these contingents represents a unique aspect of assessment.

For example, the Tech Prep concept and resulting legislation emphasizing the integration of occupational and academic learning came about in part because business determined that students were not coming into the workplace with an understanding of how their basic skills in academic areas were related to their future job responsibilities. This need has certainly not been adequately met and represents a continuing issue as legislative bodies continue to become involved in education reform initiatives throughout the country. In addition to the Tech Prep movement, there are many other groups and projects in process related to developing and assessing not only basic academic skills, but also workplace skills.

When Congress passed the Workforce Investment Act of 1998, it began what may become a trend in the way business and legislators look at funding for workforce development for secondary and postsecondary institutions and community adult education programs. Collaboration at all levels is mandated to provide the business sector with the workers it needs.

This act requires postsecondary technical colleges and community adult education programs to collaborate in what it calls a "one-stop" system of workforce investment and education opportunities. Although secondary programs are not required to participate, they can be included if state legislatures want to include them.

The demand for accountability in the education environment by citizens is another indication of continuing business involvement in assessment. This is driven primarily by the impact of economic development and will certainly continue. The National Center on Education and the Economy based in Rochester, New York, and the Learning Research and Development Center at the University of Pittsburgh in Pittsburgh, Pennsylvania, are developing a joint project called "The New Standards Project." This project adopts high national education standards and a new kind of assessment system benchmarking local assessments to national standards across the curriculum (NCRVE, 1999).

Another initiative that indicates both the future involvement of business in assessment as well as the level of concern of business for qualified personnel now and in the future is the SCANS/2000 project. This is an interdisciplinary research project at the Johns Hopkins University Institute for Policy Studies. This group is working on projects related specifically to school-to-work programs and the creation of a workforce development system that will prepare young people to compete on a global basis. The SCANS/2000 project emphasis on "career transcripts" and on the ability of a prospective employer to electronically view the qualifications of a job applicant that include both job experience and educational preparation is both visionary and revolutionary.

In recent years, the demands of the workplace have prompted the development of student standards, such as workforce readiness and job-specific skills, that extend beyond academic areas. For example, "Hawaii has developed 'work skills' standards, Michigan has developed model content standards for 'career and employability skills,' and Oklahoma has developed content standards for 'hands-on career exploration" (NCRVE, 1999).

If the product of any education system or program is inadequate, business will influence legislation to remedy the situation and develop alternative ways to hold states and local education systems accountable for outcomes. This will constitute the most significant trend in education in the future; there will be more involvement by business, not less.

Summary

If business education programs are to keep pace with emerging technologies in the workplace and maintain their viability by providing the appropriate preparation of business and industry's workforce, the involvement of business in all aspects of education management—especially assessment—will be critical. Educators need advice from the business community regarding competencies, equipment, facilities, and employability levels of its graduates. The positive results of the collaboration that can occur through the effort and initiative of the business educator with business and industry can be the defining factor in program effectiveness.

The involvement of business should not be viewed as a required aspect of legislation, but rather, it should be viewed as an opportunity for continuous feedback and improvement of the education system through outcomes assessment. Taking the approach of considering our education system as one component of a larger community—society—allows an educator to seek ways to integrate the business community for the improvement of the larger community. Business and governmental bodies have now come to the full realization that the quality of the workforce determines the quality of life for its members.

As with any other aspect of society, continuous assessment of education programs must occur from a variety of sources, involving a variety of evaluation methods and focusing on all aspects of an education program to determine its effectiveness so that improvement can be a continuous cycle. Businesses are ready and willing to participate because they understand the importance of their involvement. Business educators face the challenge of getting these rich resources in the business community involved in their programs so that the full potential of this partnership can be realized.

References

Border, B. (1998). *The status of alternative assessments through the 1990's.* Decatur, GA: Vocational–Technical Education Consortium of States, Southern Association of Colleges and Schools.

Bottoms, G. (1993). *Redesigning and refocusing high school vocational studies.* Atlanta, GA: Southern Regional Education Board.

Bottoms, G., Presson, A., & Johnson, M. (1992). *Making high schools work.* Atlanta, GA: Southern Region Education Board.

Brustein, M., & Mahler, M. (1998). *One-stop guide to the Perkins Act of 1998.* Washington, DC: Brustein and Manasevit.

Burke, K. (1994). *The mindful school: How to assess authentic learning.* Palatine, IL: IRI/Skylight Training and Publishing, Inc.

Carnevale, A. P. (1991). *America and the new economy: How new competitive standards are radically changing the American workplaces.* San Francisco: Jossey-Bass, Inc., Publishers.

Cisco networking academies program review. (1997). San Jose, CA: Cisco Systems Corporation.

Edling, W. (1992). *Creating a tech prep curriculum.* Waco, TX: Center for Occupational Research and Development.

Hudecki, P. (1999, Summer). Update on new legislation (Perkins III). *CenterWork, 10* (2).

Hull, D. (1992). *Getting started with tech prep.* Waco, TX: Center for Occupational Research and Development.

Kazis, R., & Barton, P. E. (1993). *Improving the transition from school to work in the United States.* Washington, DC: American Youth Policy Forum.

National Business Education Association. (1995). *National standards for business education: What America's students should know and be able to do in business.* Reston, VA: National Business Education Association.

National Center for Research in Vocational Education (NCRVE). (1999). *NCRVE's skill standards page* [Online]. Available: http://vocserve.berkeley.edu/SkillsPage.html

Nebraska State Board of Education Assessment Policy. (1998). Lincoln, NE: National State Board of Education.

SCANS/2000. The workforce skills website. [Online]. Available: http://www.scans.jhu.edu/

South Carolina Department of Education. (1999). *Handbook for advisory groups in career and technology education.* Columbia, SC: South Carolina Department of Education.

Enhanced Assessment Through Student Participation

Jill White and Wally Holmes Bouchillon
University of West Florida
Pensacola, Florida

Traditionally, business educators have used production assignments and paper-and-pencil tests to assess student performance in the classroom. Student participation and input can enhance the assessment process, and new approaches that involve the student have been devised. Authentic assessment, often called alternative assessment, is a method that is based on hands-on learning activities that provide an understanding of complex, real-world problems; it requires active learning and higher-level thinking from students.

This chapter will focus on four specific authentic assessment tools: portfolios, journals, peer assessment, and career assessment. They are found in the literature related to "best practices" for teaching and learning and allow students to participate as active partners in the educational process. The strategies support students as they develop and use critical-thinking, problem-solving, and decision-making skills to grade their performance on a variety of classroom tasks. Such self-assessment encourages students to take ownership and responsibility for their learning, to take risks in a supportive environment, and to negotiate ways to demonstrate their learning.

Self-assessment activities should not only examine simple recall of information, but should also determine the extent to which students have processed and will use this information. For example, can students apply what they have learned to situations that require reasoning and critical thinking? Can they use their knowledge of business technology to communicate their ideas and demonstrate their workplace competencies?

Business education is based on real-world, real-life standards of performance. Using self-assessment as part of authentic assessment activities helps reveal the extent to which students have accomplished these skills. Similar to contextual learning, which is based on a student's ability to understand and apply knowledge (Parnell, 1995), authentic assessment is application oriented. To be effective, such assessment requires a continuous effort on the part of the teacher and his or her students in refining established goals to reflect desired learning objectives.

Literature Review

The learning objectives within the business education framework call for using multiple forms of assessment to understand each student's progress and to evaluate the impact of instructional strategies. Allowing students to assess their own performance adds a nontraditional focus to the assessment process. As criteria are established for student self-assessment, teachers must coach and guide students to ensure that the assessment is authentic. Learning goals that focus on students' achievement must be established.

Schunk and Ertmer (1998) determined that students who had established learning goals enhanced their self-efficacy for successfully performing computer-based tasks. Harrington (1995) states that current use of self-assessment methodology taps more ability areas than existing ability or aptitude tests cover. Self-assessment approaches have been used to enhance student self-discovery and awareness, to promote student self-reflection and self-esteem, and to improve student outcomes.

As students participate in the assessment process, they tend to develop a feeling of ownership and pride in the assigned lesson. According to Ackerman, Hughes, and Wilder (1997), students who lack ownership in their learning tend to have high incidences of homework infractions, are extrinsically motivated, and do not accept responsibility for their learning. When students understand the criteria for good work, they are more likely to meet the established criteria. A clearer understanding of quality work can be established if students have the opportunity to participate in defining the criteria for good work.

Eisner (1999) places performance-based assessment (authentic assessment) in a "broad educational and social context." He supports the use of performance-based assessment to measure a child's ability to achieve. To survive in today's society, Eisner professes that "the kind of thinking students are now being encouraged to engage in requires much more than what Edward Thorndike dreamed of."

According to Eisner, context matters, critical thinking is crucial, and students need to be able to solve problems for themselves. He suggests that a possible solution to our current form of assessment would be to use two different types of assessment, one focused on the general and the other designed for the particular. The general assessment tool would focus on using comparative data to determine school performance. The particular assessment would be designed to reveal "the distinctive talents of individual students and the effects of school practice on their development" (p. 1).

A review of the literature suggests that student self-assessment can be used not only as a grading device, but also as a teaching strategy. As students become more active in the assessment process, they can establish new goals, identify their strengths and weaknesses, and analyze their progress. Self-assessment should be linked to practice for analysis or reflection to become meaningful. Teachers need to support their students by providing time for them to think about and evaluate their progress. Educators need to remember that the primary focus of all assessment should be providing feedback that helps students meet their learning goals.

Self-Assessment Approaches

Portfolio assessment. Portfolios are one form of authentic assessment that encourages students to develop their self-assessment skills (Imel, 1993). Portfolio assessment is a purposeful collection of a student's work that provides a long-term record of the student's best efforts, progress, and achievement in a given area. Students must participate in the selection of the materials included in the portfolio and the criteria used to assess it. Depending on the intent, portfolios serve as the basis for assessing individual student growth over time on specific standards and benchmarks.

Types of portfolios. Employment or career portfolios contain students' documented academic and workplace skills, samples of their best work, certificates of achievement, community service activities, and letters of recommendation. These portfolios may also contain grades, career interests, résumés, or other documents that students feel will represent their potential as prospective employees. Not only do employers use portfolios to evaluate an individual's abilities, but many high schools also require student portfolios for graduation. Colleges may require portfolios as a part of the admission process.

Portfolios can be used to assess learning specifically in a theme or unit of an academic and/or vocational project. For these portfolios, students must reflect on their own learning by evaluating their strengths, weaknesses, or ways to improve their performance on specific assignments. Performance is directly related to accomplished practices that are used in many states to determine student performance. Portfolios may be used to provide documentation that a student has mastered those practices.

Portfolios also encourage self-directed learning. Self-directed learners are able to prioritize and achieve goals, monitor and assess their own progress, and assume responsibility for their learning. Students are given the freedom to use portfolios to develop research interests, assess their own knowledge base and performance, and play a constructive role in illuminating matters that are significant to them.

Research collaboration with fellow classmates is another important use of portfolio assessment. Students share research ideas, constructive criticism, and coherence in research investigations. They begin to respect and listen to each other's ideas in an honest, unassuming manner. They also provide each other with critical feedback that alters the classroom culture from a competitive atmosphere to one of interactive communication and considerate behavior during discussions.

While a portfolio can be used as an effective instructional tool, its use as an assessment instrument demands clear understanding of its purpose, specification of the desired portfolio contents, and definition of the rating methods for the individual components. Grading criteria and the purpose of the portfolio should be clearly outlined and determined by the teacher and the student. Once the criteria have been established, teachers need to provide students with a rubric (a grading scale) before the portfolio development process begins. The rubric should identify the type of information to be placed in the portfolio as well as how the portfolio will be assessed. Table 1 illustrates a rubric that can be used or adapted for portfolio development and assessment.

Table 1. Example of Portfolio Rubric

Item	Possible Points	Student Assessment	Teacher Assessment
Professional Binder	10		
Cover Sheet	10		
Table of Contents	10		
Résumé	10		
Career Assessment Activities	10		
Completed Projects	10		
Self-Directed Learning Activities	10		
Examples of Reflective Practice	10		
Research Activities	10		
Certificates / Awards	10		
Total Points	100		

Student outcomes are critical in the assessment process. Identified outcomes of portfolio assessment in the business classroom include the following:

- Students can become self-directed learners through the use of portfolios.
- Portfolio assessment involves peer evaluation that enhances interactive communication and consideration for other students.
- Portfolio assessment gives the student the opportunity to become a quality researcher.
- Through the use of portfolios, students' thought processes involve integration of information to assess and resolve issues critical to their lives.

When portfolio assessment is designed and implemented properly, assessment is continuous, collaborative, multidimensional, grounded in knowledge, and authentic (Valeri-Gold, Olson, and Demming, December 1991–January 1992).

Journals. The use of journals has its foundation in cognitive behavior theories. Rational emotive theory (RET) uses journals in assisting clients to become aware of their modes of thinking, their self-concepts, and the way in which they process information. Individuals are asked to put their thoughts on paper; the entries are then used to identify overall themes and patterns. Journals in the educational area can be used in the same manner.

Journals, writing conferences, reflection logs, teacher-student interviews, and self-assessment checklists and inventories all require students to evaluate their work, determine what they have learned, and identify possible areas that remain unclear. These self-assessment techniques are a form of record keeping in which students respond in writing to specific probes or questions from the teacher or from their peers. The probes focus student responses on knowledge or skills specific to a standard or benchmark.

Journal writing has many different formats. Dialogue journals, for example, are used to record conversations between students or between teachers and students. These journals require students to develop listening and oral communication skills in addition to reading and writing skills. Using dialogue journals is also an effective strategy to emphasize meaning in a given assignment. Students are allowed to freely respond to the effectiveness or relevancy of an assignment.

Double-entry journals and personal journals are used to record students' educational experiences as well as their personal insights. In double-entry journals (which are similar to double-entry accounting), the pages of the journal are divided into two columns; different information is then recorded in each column. Information may include specific items such as quotes from a text in one column and the students' response to the text in the other.

Journals can be used as a strategy to develop structured writing. Writing about assigned topics on a regular basis can help develop communication and writing skills such as proper syntax and grammar. Journals increase student interest and participation; they provide continuous feedback from the teacher to help establish positive relationships between the teacher and the student. Business education students are encouraged to use journals to document progress on projects, to conduct self-directed Internet searches, and to record their learning experiences. Through the use of journals, students use critical-thinking skills, demonstrate personal accountability for their learning, and develop research and resource-management skills.

When journals are used to assess student projects, the entries are of a more reflective nature. Students identify their strengths, weaknesses, frustrations, successes, and accomplishments as they complete the assignment. The actual learning process is documented. Students can evaluate and improve their performance through the self-evaluation or reflective practice process.

Reflective practice is also evident in journals used to identify workplace related learning experiences. Students who participate in job shadowing, mentoring, cooperative education, or work-based experiences use journals to identify job skills and personal characteristics needed to become successful employees. Students' personal reflections provide insight for career choices and improvement of inter- and intrapersonal skills as students prepare to bridge the gap between school and work.

Teachers should assist students with the development of guidelines for entering information into journals. Without definite or detailed criteria, students may not use journals in the most beneficial manner. Entries should be evaluated weekly to provide students valuable and practical feedback.

Through journal writing, students explore their thinking processes, use their imaginations, and share experiences with fellow students. Journals of accomplishments can also be used informally to assess the development of business skills. As with portfolios, these self-assessment tools become effective when they are organized and evaluated using specific criteria.

Peer assessment. Relatively little research has been conducted on peer assessment. Little evidence is provided that peer assessment is actually used in a "systematic manner." Rosbottom (1994) states that although peer marking is used a great deal, actual peer assessment is limited because it requires assessor training and an organized environment to be effective.

Peer assessment can be described as students evaluating each other's work using objective criteria. By assessing the work of their classmates, students often see alternative reasoning patterns and develop an appreciation for diverse ways of approaching and solving problems. Because peer assessment is used in business and industry to improve performance, its use in the classroom can help students develop the critical-thinking, problem-solving, interpersonal, and communication skills that they will need in the workplace.

Peer assessment may be conducted individually or in groups. If group assessment is used, students' concerns relating to this method must be addressed. These concerns include not having time to conduct group work other than during school hours and having their grade dependent upon the abilities and efforts of others. To address these concerns, teachers must provide in-class time to work on group projects. Specific group-assessment forms that allow students to assess contributions of each group member, provide practice for student assessment, and provide both quantitative and qualitative assessment can be used effectively to decrease student concerns (Bulman, 1996).

Integrated learning projects that have both written and project-based components are excellent examples of assignments where peer assessment is effective. For written projects, students proofread, analyze sentence structure, and identify grammatical errors in the documents. Once a peer has evaluated the document, the written assignment is returned to the student for correction. After all corrections have been completed, the teacher receives the document for final evaluation. The same techniques can be used to evaluate a project such as a student newspaper, a poster presentation, or a PowerPoint presentation.

Videotaping a student's oral presentation can be used to improve his or her communication skills. Students view their tapes and critique their own performance before their fellow students provide feedback. Predesigned cards with the identified grading criteria can be given to students to assess each other. The cards can be signed by each student or completed anonymously. Students should be encouraged to give sound constructive criticism so that their classmates can improve their presentation skills.

Whether peer assessment is used to assess students on an individual or a group basis, for project-based activities, or for student presentations, this technique should not be used as a final evaluation of a student's ability to complete an assignment. Many times students have a tendency to be biased toward other students; they may be either too lenient with their friends or too critical of individuals they do not know. Teachers must play an active role in assisting students in determining grading criteria. Table 2 provides an example of a self-assessment tool for students to identify how well they have contributed to a group project.

Career assessment. Before students can make reliable career and life decisions, they must first assess themselves. This process includes becoming aware of their interests, values, skills, and lifestyle preferences. Self-assessment

Table 2. Self-Evaluation

1. Was I present for all classes? If not, was it for a good reason?
2. Was I on time for all classes?
3. Did I turn in my assignments on time?
4. Did I participate in class discussion? Too much? Too little?
5. Did I ask questions when I was confused?
6. Did I study, as I should have?
7. Can I apply what I learned?
8. What could I have done differently to make myself a better student?
9. Was I an active participant in my group?
10. If you had to grade yourself, what grade would you assign?

practices provide information to individuals about their emotional, intellectual, and social-growth experiences.

Career assessment has been used in guidance and counseling for a number of years. Peterson, Sampson, and Reardon state that "self-knowledge and occupational knowledge consist of sets of organized memory structures called schemata that evolve over a person's life span" (1991, p. 7). Therefore, for students to be able to choose a career, they must be able to evaluate their interests, skills, and preferences for a given vocation. It is also important for students to understand the basic educational requirements for the degree programs they choose.

In their book, *Career Development and Services: A Cognitive Approach*, Peterson, Sampson, and Reardon (1991) identify the phases of CASVE, which is used in career counseling. This sequential system incorporates the use of communication, analysis, synthesis, valuing, and execution (CASVE) for identifying career choices.

Zunker's Dimension of Life-Style Orientation Survey (DLOS) (1994), the Self-Directed Search (SDS) based on Holland's (1992) theory of career development, and the Strong Interest Inventory (SII) (1983) are all career selection inventories that are student self-administered. These inventories are popular with students of all ages.

Inventories are designed to identify activities that relate to various careers or occupations. The rationale is that "individuals having similar interest patterns to those found in an occupational group would probably find satisfaction in that particular group" (Zunker and Norris, 1998). Through the use of these self-directed searches, students become comfortable assessing their strengths and weaknesses, identifying their likes and dislikes, and selecting the career that would most satisfy their interests and abilities.

Self-directed searches appear in written format, such as pamphlets and workbooks, as well as computer software. High school career centers or career labs provide students the opportunity to conduct self-directed career analysis by using such programs as Discover, a self-directed computer guide that consists of nine modules. Once students complete the interests and values section of the modules, an extensive list of occupations relating to the student's identified interest is provided. The list of occupations provides descriptions of the various careers, salaries for the occupations, and training that is necessary for students to enter a given profession.

MIDAS, the Multiple Intelligences Developmental Assessment Scales, is another example of a self-assessment instrument that is available to students. This particular instrument is based on the theory of multiple intelligences. Questions asked include inquiries about a student's everyday life, involvement, and judgment. According to Shearer (1997), MIDAS provides "information that is useful for increasing self-awareness regarding skills and abilities" as they relate to multiple intelligences.

SIGI Plus provides students a complete, self-directed, interactive software system to identify career guidance information. Educational Testing Services (ETS) developed this program to help students clarify work-related values. Students can obtain up-to-date information on numerous occupations, determine educational and training requirements for those occupations, and design a career plan that fits their specific career goals.

The Internet is also a useful tool for exploring career options. However, students need to use a variety of search engines to locate jobs in a vocation they are interested in pursuing. Many job applications or college entrance applications are online. Students should be encouraged to use the Internet to complete these applications. Once the searches have been completed, they can use the information to provide a written summary of their findings. Additional Internet practices and research activities include searches for salary surveys, tips on preparing career portfolios, identifying relocation information, and designing résumés.

Prospective employers search résumés for keywords that identify specific qualities candidates possess. Assessment tools can be designed to evaluate the effectiveness of a student's résumé. Students and teachers can design check sheets to ensure that students include pertinent information on their résumés. Tailoring a résumé to meet the needs of the employer is a crucial skill students need to develop. Including keywords, targeted vocabulary, and industry termi-nology from an employer's job description helps students design résumés that will market their skills.

Unfortunately, many students are not aware of the skills they possess. Therefore, they need a more comprehensive career assessment. Self-awareness, experience, previous testing, and personal goals all are factors that must be taken into consideration when selecting career assessment instruments. Changes in career education theory and practice require that if students are to be successful in today's society, they must develop a broader understanding of the importance of career development throughout their lives.

Once students identify their career development needs, guidance programs that are geared to address these needs must be developed and managed. Gysbers (1995) states that guidance programs "need to emphasize perceptual learning activities during elementary school, conceptual learning activities during middle school and junior high, and generalization learning activities during high school" (p. 1).

Summary

The utilization of new assessment strategies is essential to continued improvement of classroom assessment. As teaching practices change, assessment methodology must also change to ensure relevant and useful feedback. The four assessment strategies provided in this chapter have been identified in the literature as best practices. Through the use of portfolio development, journal entries, peer assessment, and career assessment, students develop a more clear and concise understanding of the skills they will need to be successful in their chosen careers. In addition to providing a better understanding of the workplace skills needed in business and industry, each of these assessment strategies gives students the opportunity to participate in the design of their own assessment. By participating in the development of the criteria for assessment, students develop a sense of ownership, pride, and responsibility in their educational success.

Assessment in business education has a multitude of formats. Whether educators use traditional formats, which include paper-and-pencil tests, or they use nontraditional formats, such as the ones provided here, the primary concern of all assessment should be successful student performance. Student performance can be positively influenced if the assessments used are directly related to the skills that business and industry will require them to demonstrate.

References

Ackerman, S. L., Hughes, L., & Wilder, R. (1997). *Improving student responsibility*. Master's Action Research Project, Saint Xavier University. (ERIC Document Reproduction Service No. ED 411 957)

Bulman, T. (1996, Spring). *Peer assessment in group work*. [Online]. Available: http://www.oaa.pdx.edu/CAE/FacultyFocus

Eisner, E. W. (1999, May). The uses and limits of performance assessment. *Phi Delta Kappan Online* [Online]. Available: http://pdkint.org/kappan/keis990\\5.htm

Gysbers, N. C. (1995, September-October). *Youth career planning—Career development knows no boundaries*. Paper presented at the International

Convention for Education, Training, and Development, Port Douglas, Queensland, Australia.

Harrington, T. F. (1995). *Assessment of abilities*. ERIC Clearinghouse on Counseling and Student Services, University of North Carolina. (Report No. CG 025961).

Holland, J. L. (1992). *Making vocational choices* (2nd ed.). Odessa, FL: Psychological Assessment Resources.

Imel, S. (1993). *Portfolio assessment in adult, career, and vocational education. Trends and issues alert*. Columbus, OH: ERIC Clearinghouse.

Levitt, J. (1999, December). *Navigating the net for job search & career success*. Presentation at the National Conference of the Association for Career and Technical Education (ACTE), Orlando, FL.

Parnell, D. (1995). *Why do I have to learn this? Teaching the way children learn best*. Waco, TX: Center for Occupational Research and Development.

Peterson, G. W., Sampson, J. P., & Reardon, R. C. (1991). *Career development and services: A cognitive approach*. Pacific Grove, CA: Brooks/Cole.

Rosbottom, J. (1994). *Software tools for peer assessment*. Paper presented at CTI Annual Conference, Dublin City University, Dublin, Ireland.

Schunk, D. H., & Ertmer, P. A. (1998, August). *Self-evaluation and self-regulated computer learning*. Paper presented at the Annual Meeting of the American Psychological Association (106th), San Francisco.

Shearer, C. B. (1997, August). *Reliability, validity, and utility of a multiple intelligences assessment for career planning*. Paper presented at the Annual Meeting of the American Psychological Association (105th), Chicago.

Strong, E. K. (1983). *Vocational interest bank for men*. Stanford, CA: Stanford University Press.

Valeri-Gold, M., Olson, J. R., & Demming, M. P. (December 1991–January 1992). Portfolios: Collaborative authentic assessment opportunities for college developmental learners. *Journal of Reading, 35* (4), 298–305.

Zunker, V. G. (1994). *Using assessment results for career development* (4th ed.). Pacific Grove, CA: Brooks/Cole.

Zunker, V. G., & Norris, D. S. (1998). *Using assessment results for career development*. Pacific Grove, CA: Brooks/Cole.

New Assessment Strategies to Improve Business Teacher Preparation

Betty J. Brown
Ball State University
Muncie, Indiana

Since 1983, when *A Nation at Risk* called attention to the lack of student preparation for the demands of the workplace, the U.S. education system has been criticized on many fronts. One focus of this criticism has been the knowledge and skills of teachers. A recent movement to improve teacher preparation has extensively changed education programs. Emphasis in the current movement is on "performance-based assessment" as a measure of the competencies that will enable a teacher to handle classroom responsibilities. In business teacher education, as in all other areas of teacher preparation, curriculum reform is underway.

New Assessment Standards

Initiatives for change in teacher preparation have a wide range of origins (Palomba and Banta, 1999). National, regional, state, and local curriculum standards; a national assessment movement; and professional teaching standards for different content areas each have dramatic implications for prospective teachers. These standards require that teachers demonstrate competence in their subjects in more direct ways than they did in the past. They also require the development of skill in using performance-based assessment strategies, so that no major gap exists between the policy demands of teacher and student performance, and the ability of teachers to measure up to those standards. Thus, teacher education, including business education, must respond to all these initiatives in a timely and effective manner.

Current practice sometimes places a new teacher in the school without continuing assistance in managing the classroom. Curriculum guides, course competencies, and content standards provide direction about subject matter, but the other aspects of classroom management may be a challenge. In many schools, mentoring programs have provided guidance from experienced colleagues to help new teachers cope with student diversity, classroom management problems, and the context of their teaching. One objective of new assessment standards is to assure assistance to new teachers in all aspects of teaching; mentoring and a program of induction will provide ongoing support.

In his classic book, *Basic Principles of Curriculum and Instruction,* Tyler (1949) first outlined the importance of carefully defining educational objectives as a core concept for curriculum development. His rationale for curriculum development revolved around these central questions:

- What educational purposes should the school seek to attain?
- Which educational experiences will most likely attain these purposes?
- How can these educational experiences be effectively organized?
- By what means can we determine whether these purposes are being attained?

Tyler considered the first question the most crucial step in the process of curriculum development, since the other three steps follow from it in terms of determining the goals of the schools' programs. As a result of the educational reform movement of the past decade, educational programs at all levels have re-evaluated answers to these three questions for schools of the 21st century. Like educational programs, business teacher educators have evaluated processes for teacher preparation. Training prospective business teachers for all facets of their classroom experiences in the future is critical.

Business Teacher Education and Performance-Based Assessment

The educational purposes of business teacher education can be defined by answering the question, "What should prospective business education teachers be able to do, and how can they demonstrate that they can do it satisfactorily?" That premise is at the heart of the performance-based assessment system defined by the National Professional Standards Board, the Interstate New Teacher Assessment and Support Consortium (INTASC), and state professional standards boards.

Traditional teacher education programs have relied on completion of course work and a minimal overall grade point average as criteria for completion. Completion of such a program may or may not lead to licensure. Other state requirements, such as a licensing examination, must have been met. Performance-based assessment moves a teacher education student beyond traditional evaluation methods, requiring more self-evaluation, more reflection on what has been learned, and a search for ways to use newer evaluation techniques in a performance-based assessment process.

One of the forces driving teacher education reform, or the application of new standards and assessment procedures to teacher education, is the belief that the completion of courses, even with excellent grades, does not verify competence. Professional standards boards have the objective of assuring that students are assessed throughout their teacher preparation programs in subject matter and teaching competence. Based on those assessments, students may progress to the next level, may complete additional educational experiences as "remediation," or may be terminated from the program. Performance-based assessment requires prospective teachers to be evaluated and measured against professional standards as identified by national, regional, and state standards boards.

A business teacher education program based on performance-based assessment requires prospective teachers to learn how to plan instruction to meet their objectives and to carry out all activities of a teacher with skill and insight. A business teacher education program should be able to report to school systems that will employ their graduates that prospective teachers have met state performance assessment standards, many of which have a common core of INTASC standards.

The INTASC Core Standards

The INTASC standards, on which state standards are usually based, include three broad areas of competencies necessary for all teachers in schools of the 21st century: knowledge, skills or performance, and disposition.

Knowledge standards. Teachers must understand principles and theories of student development, understand how individual differences between students influence their behavior and learning, value the uniqueness of each student, and know how to create learning activities that take into consideration the developmental characteristics of all students.

Skill or performance standards. Prospective teachers must demonstrate that they can create learning opportunities and positive classroom environments, as well as adapt curriculum, instruction, resources, and assessment tools so that all students can learn.

Disposition standards. Teachers must exhibit a commitment to their profession and to their students. They must respect the range of individual differences among their students and hold high but realistic expectations for their behavior and learning. Commitment to establishing a caring learning environment and to working with the families and others to promote healthy student development are additional requirements. Teachers must also value the principles and research of good teaching, the opportunity of working with a diverse population, and the importance of all who influence the learning process. These standards related to disposition identify teacher qualities that have always been valued but in many ways have not been assessed in a systematic way.

The 10 INTASC model core standards address the following specific areas:

1. Content knowledge;
2. Intellectual, social, and personal development of learners;
3. Ability to work with diverse learners;
4. Development of critical-thinking, problem-solving, and performance skills;
5. Use of instructional strategies that create a positive learning environment;
6. Effective verbal, nonverbal, and media communication;
7. Planning and integration of instruction;
8. Use of formal and informal evaluation strategies for the continuous intellectual, social, and physical development of the learner;
9. Reflective practice and the seeking out of opportunities to grow professionally; and
10. Participation in the larger community to support students' learning and well-being.

A document with all 10 standards and performance indicators for knowledge, skill or performance, and disposition is available at http://www.ccsso.org/intasc.html.

Meeting the Standards

The INTASC principles are based on the premise that a teacher is a lifelong learner—that skills in these 10 areas will be refined throughout a teaching career through professional development activities. However, a beginning teacher must demonstrate at least a basic competency in all these areas.

In all their business and general education classes, for example, teacher candidates will gather evidence for their teaching portfolios that demonstrates knowledge of the content they will teach, skills in working with diverse students in a variety of settings, and dispositions that are identified as "good teacher" characteristics.

Assessment throughout the preparation program will provide feedback on development of subject matter knowledge, teaching competence, and disposition. In methods courses, assessment procedures will be planned as part of the total assessment process. For example, early field experiences will provide opportunities for students to hone their skills and develop portfolios to demonstrate their progress toward meeting the assessment standards.

In their field experiences, teacher candidates can videotape their actual performance in the classroom. The videotapes, as well as the students' reflective thinking about the teaching and learning processes, become part of the evidence of progress. The development of written lesson plans, an important assignment in a methods course, can be followed by actual teaching of the lesson, evaluation of that teaching, and reflection on the part of the writer about the strengths and weaknesses of the written plan.

The INTASC standards require that prospective teachers thoroughly understand the discipline or disciplines they plan to teach. Teachers must also be able to create learning experiences that make the subject matter meaningful. Such skill implies a deeper knowledge of content initially, and a continual updating of knowledge—truly "lifelong learning."

National Standards for Business Education

In what content areas must business teachers be competent? The *National Standards for Business Education*, developed by the National Business Education Association (NBEA), is a guide to curriculum and competencies for teaching business courses. These standards were developed as a response to the call for national standards for performance-based assessment systems, and they define and delineate the areas of business education for the future.

The standards stress problem-solving and higher-order-thinking skills, active learning, and preparation for the workplace. Twelve areas of the business education curriculum are defined in the standards: accounting, business law, career development, communications, computation, economics and personal finance, entrepreneurship education, information systems, international business, management, marketing, and interrelationships of business functions. Emphasis in the standards for these 12 areas is on relationships among the many facets of business. Students must think, make decisions, problem solve, and apply their knowledge from all areas of their education; the business education curriculum encourages development of these skills. In turn, teacher education programs must equip teachers for a curriculum that emphasizes those competencies and skills.

Developmental Standards as Part of a Performance-Based Assessment System

Inherent in performance-based assessment systems are competencies of teachers to work with students at various grade levels and ages: early childhood, middle childhood, early adolescence, and adolescence and young adulthood. Developmental standards at each of these levels require that prospective teachers demonstrate an understanding of and ability to work with a diverse student population. For example, they must understand human development and provide appropriate opportunities to foster student growth; create, modify, and implement integrated, meaningful curricula; and plan and implement instruction based on knowledge of students, learning theory, subject matter, curricular goals, and community.

Prospective teachers must also understand the importance of multiple assessments (informal and formal, formative and summative) and use a variety of developmentally appropriate assessments to improve student learning. They must demonstrate professionalism through collegiality, peer support, and professional self-assessment; understand how children learn; and create a learning environment that supports all children and their development. In addition, they must develop and maintain positive working relationships with families, school colleagues, support services, and community members at large to support children in their learning. Actively engaging in professional growth and development in order to revitalize the professional role of teachers and student learning is also essential.

A Model for a Performance-Based Assessment System

If a performance-based system is the foundation for business teacher preparation, a prospective teacher might follow a pattern like the one shown in Figure 1. This model for teacher education is similar to many programs for teacher preparation across the country, with the INTASC standards as a base. Students must demonstrate by the end of their teacher preparation program that they have developed competencies in the 10 INTASC principles. In this model, an assessment committee monitors progress toward meeting the INTASC standards.

As early as possible in the freshman year, or at the earliest point a student declares his or her intention of becoming a teacher, the student will receive standards, expectations, and directions for beginning an assessment portfolio. Three times during a program, the student is formally evaluated by an assessment committee, which includes one or more business educators, public school personnel, content specialists, and other teacher educators, and is given feedback about all aspects of preparation for a teaching career. (For example, the Indiana Professional Standards Board Web site, http://www.state.in.us/psb, includes sets of standards for subject matter areas and developmental levels from early childhood to young adulthood.)

When students leave the university at the end of the program shown in this model, they must complete a two-year induction program with mentoring by experienced teachers in all aspects of the teaching experience. They then continue to develop their professional portfolio with evidence of their growth as teachers. Each teacher successfully completing the induction program, as judged by supervisors and fellow educators who have been trained as evaluators, is granted a "proficient practitioner" license. Assessment criteria includes a portfolio with work that demonstrates competence in knowledge, skills, and dispositions important to good teaching and effective learning.

The practitioner's license will be renewable every five years, based on performance assessments by a board of experienced teachers trained as evaluators. Still more performance assessment occurs when a proficient practitioner seeks National Board certification. This certification process requires a teacher to have completed a baccalaureate degree with at least three years' teaching experience. After applying for certification, a teacher develops and submits a portfolio demonstrating competence and then completes assessment center exercises, developed by the National Board for Professional Teaching Standards. These exercises demonstrate knowledge, skills, and abilities in the certification field. (The Web site for the National Board, http://www.nbpts.org/ nbpts/standards, provides information about certification.)

National Board certification grants an "accomplished practitioner" license, which is renewed every 10 years by demonstration of continued mastery of knowledge, skills, and dispositions. Therefore, performance assessments will occur throughout the educator's career.

In order to demonstrate competence by the time they enter teaching full time, prospective candidates must be in schools with students, applying what they are learning, developing their skills in working with diverse students in all settings, and being evaluated on progress toward the goals of their teacher education program. Early education experiences are necessary. A part of those experiences will be assistance by skilled and knowledgeable in-service teachers and college and university personnel, so that the prospective teachers receive feedback and guidance. If they are unable to demonstrate the competencies, they will be terminated from the teacher education program.

Assessing the Progress of Prospective Teachers

As prospective teachers begin the professional education program described in Figure 1, they will be required to meet with an assessment committee, present their portfolios and writing and reflection samples for evaluation, and receive feedback and perhaps remedial directives. Throughout the course work and field experiences, instructors provide opportunities for them to build their knowledge, skills, and dispositions as specified by the INTASC standards. Those instructors provide feedback and verification that students are progressing, and evidence of that progress can be added to the professional portfolio.

Prior to student teaching, substantive field experiences are part of the program. The assessment committee also verifies progress and readiness for this culminating experience. At the end of the program, the assessment committee finally evaluates evidence of attainment of basic competencies in all 10 INTASC areas, and the prospective teacher is ready to accept a teaching position and begin the two-year induction period.

Evaluation instruments for use in the entire teacher preparation process must be suitable for measuring competency for the INTASC standards. A number of researchers have attempted to develop instruments for this performance-based assessment. A study of student teacher evaluation by Hartsough, Perez, and Swain (1998) provided assistance in defining suitable assessment tools for observations of teaching. The researchers investigated assessments of

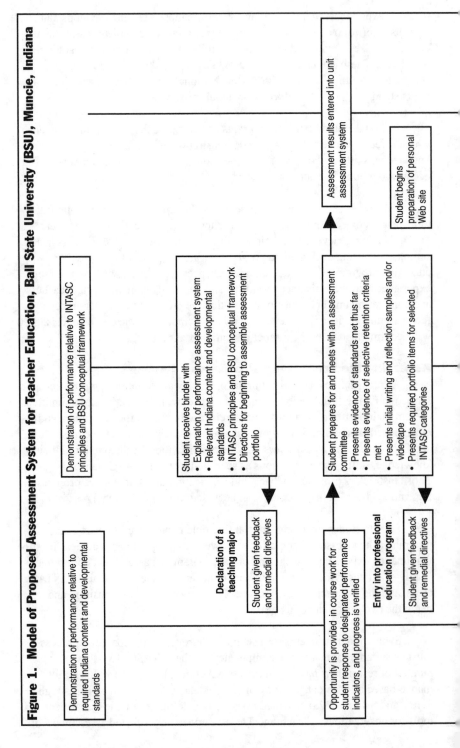

Figure 1. Model of Proposed Assessment System for Teacher Education, Ball State University (BSU), Muncie, Indiana

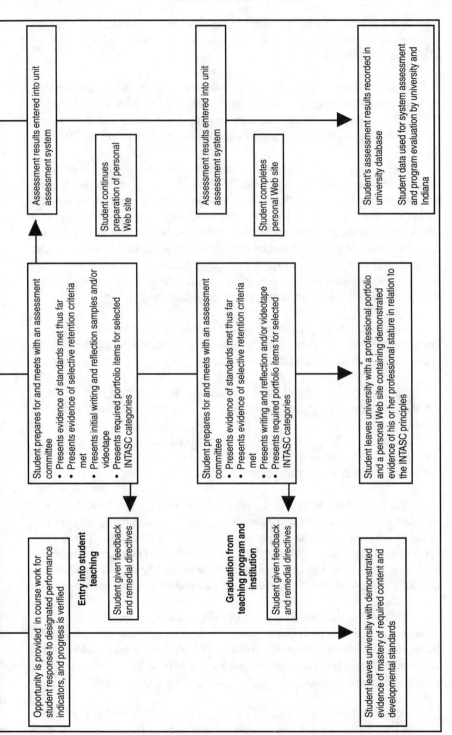

teacher behavior and found two common types: a behavior-based, low-inference observation system and a high-inference rating system. Both are based on classroom observation.

A low-inference observation system overlooks teacher attributes that cannot be measured by counting the number of times certain discrete behaviors occur. These systems do not appraise such qualities of teacher effectiveness as organizational ability, participation in school life, subject-matter knowledge, and interest.

High-inference rating systems can be among the most reliable and valid assessment techniques, depending on the format of their presentation and the care and skill used in their preparation. The researchers used six domains that were the assessment component of the California Standards for the Teaching Profession. These domains address whether a teacher accomplishes the following: creates and maintains an environment for student learning, understands and organizes content for student learning, plans instruction and designs learning experiences for all students, engages all students in powerful learning, assesses student learning, and develops as a professional to improve teaching and learning.

Five central concepts in the national teaching certification standards correlate well with these six domains. Those five central concepts, identified as typifying good teaching practices, are

- Responsibility for managing and monitoring student learning,
- Knowledge of the subjects taught and how to teach those subjects to the students,
- Systematic thinking about teaching practices and learning from experience,
- Commitment to students and their learning, and
- Membership in learning communities.

The researchers collected a sample of behavior descriptors for each of the six preservice teaching attributes, selected the most valid subset of those descriptors, and assigned scale values to each descriptor in the subset. Their process resulted in rating scales with descriptors fairly evenly distributed across the six attributes. Their next step was to introduce three general benchmark statements to characterize the least, moderate, and most effective performance levels.

This project illustrated the value of using a scaling process to develop rating components for performance-based assessment systems. Can this process be applied to business teacher preparation? The six broad areas could be part of an assessment tool for evaluating prospective teachers as they finish their preservice experiences and get ready for full-time teaching positions.

Feedback for any performance-based assessment has a goal of providing enough information for a teacher to know how well he or she did, what was done well, and which areas need improvement and in what ways. Rubrics are one way of providing more feedback than just a letter or numeric grade. For example, a four-level rubric might include these criteria for presentations:

- Highest level: Clearly organized
- Level 3: Organized
- Level 2: Somewhat organized, but disorganized in part
- Level 1: Disorganized

Ideally, evaluations will include comments that give further help to a student for improvement. An example of a rubric that provides feedback on dispositions is:

- Highest level: Worked with all students in an equitable, effective, and caring manner
- Level 3: Worked with most students in an equitable, effective, and caring manner
- Level 2: Did not demonstrate to a few students an equitable, effective, and caring manner
- Level 1: Failed to demonstrate an equitable, effective, and caring manner toward students

Feedback would include comments, as well as a summative evaluation such as "excellent," "proficient," or "basic" competency. Rubrics help teacher educators make judgments about students' knowledge, skill in instruction, and dispositions toward students and teaching. If used properly, they provide feedback for a student to be able to identify strengths and weaknesses and areas for improvement.

Multiple measures of student performance are essential to a balanced approach to monitoring and evaluation. Evaluation of portfolios, observations with feedback, evaluation with rubrics of written work and performance, evaluation of students' reflective thinking, and self-evaluation are ways in which a performance-based assessment system can help prospective teachers prepare for the classroom.

Business Teacher Preparation Based on a Performance-Based Assessment System

All the education reform movements and standards provided by various agencies emphasize a major task for business teacher educators. They must sort out what should be part of the preservice education program, what can best be learned through guided practice in someone else's classroom (in partnerships with teachers in schools), and what is best learned "on the job" as a classroom teacher.

The *National Standards for Business Education* is an excellent guide for business education content knowledge. Professional knowledge and skills must be taught in content courses and methods courses, but they can be enhanced by extensive, early field experiences with feedback from veteran educators who use the INTASC principles for guidance and evaluation of prospective teachers. Additional qualities, sensibilities, attitudes, and commitments are important. These dispositions, or tendencies or inclinations to act in particular ways, combine a prospective teacher's abilities with his or her desire to teach well.

What will a performance-based business teacher education program include? Much of the assessment will be in terms of "what can a prospective business teacher do, and how can the teacher demonstrate what he or she can do?" Early experiences for a prospective teacher will provide opportunities to become acquainted with what a teacher does and to demonstrate knowledge, skills, and dispositions in the classroom.

One of the products of a business education program will be a portfolio, evidence of learning what a teacher does. For example, a business teacher will be able to provide lesson plans, teaching materials, class projects and assign-ments, and reflective thinking about all these tasks; formal tests and quizzes; writing samples from students; evidence of attendance and participation at professional meetings, presentations, and/or workshops; records of civic involve-ment; documentation of conferences with parents/guardians; and documentation of use of community agencies. The teacher education program must provide multiple opportunities for students to demonstrate their competence, and then document that competence through evidence that can be evaluated and measured against the INTASC standards.

If preservice teacher education provided a strong foundation in subject matter and pedagogy, what kinds of learning would new teachers still need? One of the outcomes of a performance-based assessment system ideally will be beginning teachers whose preparation is strong and who have undergone experiences that have enabled them to refine their teaching knowledge and skills more than beginning teachers did in the past. When they are ready to begin full-time teaching, mentors and other fellow teachers in the schools can help them to learn "on the job" or as part of the induction phase of their careers. "Apprenticeships" with experienced teachers will provide the learning and guidance they need.

If grades and completion of courses are not to be the sole measure of competence, teacher education faculties and students must be aware of opportu-nities for multiple assessments of knowledge, skills, performance, and disposi-tions. What additional assessment tools can be used? In content courses, students should be aware of the need to observe teaching methods, techniques, and materials used in all of their classroom and field experiences. Very early in their program, they should begin to build their portfolios as evidence of their competence. In content courses, instructors should provide opportunities for and verification of student responses to performance indicators. In early field experiences, students can demonstrate a growing awareness of all the tasks of a teacher, interact with learners, and focus on demonstrating that they are building their skill in meeting content and developmental standards.

Many teacher preparation programs already include aspects of performance-based assessment. For example, business education methods students have long been required to visit classrooms, observe students, record their impressions in journals, and present a lesson to the students. They have then completed a supervised student teaching experience, with regular observations, feedback, and evaluation by master teachers. Their performance often has been assessed through the use of instruments that evaluate them on their behaviors; performance; subject matter knowledge; competence in working with all types of students; and ability to use rating scales or rubrics, which give more feedback than just a grade. Performance-based assessment may mean primarily a refinement in some evaluative processes, with students providing more reflective thinking about their experience than is evidenced in other evaluative processes.

A key to a performance-based assessment system that will truly help prospective teachers develop the knowledge, skills, and dispositions they need is a plan that provides early opportunities for students to set goals. Then they should be given frequent and helpful feedback throughout the program and assistance in developing the competencies they will need, not only for teaching, but also for providing evidence of their competence throughout their careers.

Examples of performance indicators that demonstrate that a teacher education candidate "knows and can do" what is needed in a performance-based assessment system are

- Differentiated lesson plans demonstrating a variety of teaching strategies;
- Samples of student work;
- Videotaped examples of the teacher at work and of student performances;
- Sample tests, lists of materials used in teaching, samples of checklists used to record development;
- Collection of pre- and posttest data, with interpretative narrative explaining a plan for implementing changes in instruction based on the data;
- Collection of work samples showing growth, tests, and samples of student questions;
- A management plan;
- Examples of communication with parents explaining a plan for managing the classroom environment to create positive, active engagement in learning;
- Observation checklists;
- Formal tests, quizzes, writing samples from students;

- Evidence of attendance at/participation in professional meetings, presentations, and/or workshops;
- Records of civic involvement;
- Documentation of conferences with parents/guardians; and
- Use of community agencies.

Summary

In describing a new mission for education, Darling-Hammond and Cobb (1996) included a number of teacher responsibilities. Educators must prepare all students to think critically; to frame problems; to find, integrate, and synthesize information; to create new solutions; to learn on their own; and to work cooperatively. Teachers must also understand cognition and the many different pathways to learning. They must understand child development and pedagogy as well as the structure of subject areas and a variety of alternatives for assessing learning. Education will require substantially more knowledge and radically different skills for teachers, as changes occur in the way schools operate.

Central to a performance-based assessment system is evidence that a teacher is able to demonstrate skill in working with and interacting with students, in promoting students' teamwork skills and attitudes, in analyzing and evaluating students' participation, and in reflecting on teaching practice. These skills must be developed in teachers as part of their teacher preparation program if they are to be able to meet local, state, and national standards. State standards are built on the premise that a teacher's preparation is not complete at the end of the preservice program; skills and knowledge continue to develop throughout the induction period and after.

New emphasis on performance-based assessment in teacher education brings change and challenge to business teacher education. As performance-based assessment systems are initiated, prospective teachers will need early experiences to enable them to build their teaching skills and gather evidence of progress toward achieving the levels of subject matter competence, teaching skill, and dispositions for teaching that INTASC and state standards mandate. Early experiences will enable them to practice their knowledge and skill development. By the end of their preservice preparation, these new business teachers will be able to demonstrate the competencies that will enable them to progress in their chosen careers.

References

Annual report to Indiana professional standards board. (1998, October). Unpublished Manuscript, Ball State University Teachers College, Muncie, IN.

Darling-Hammond, L. (1997). *The right to learn.* San Francisco: Jossey-Bass Inc., Publishers.

Darling-Hammond, L. (1998). Teacher learning that supports student learning. *Educational Leadership, 55* (5), 6–11.

Darling-Hammond, L., & Cobb, V. (1996). The changing context of teacher education. In F. B. Murray (Ed.), *The teacher educator's handbook: Building a knowledge base for the preparation of teachers* (p. 14). San Francisco: Jossey-Bass Inc., Publishers.

Hartsough, C. S., Perez, K. D., & Swain, C. L. (1998). Development and scaling of a preservice teacher rating instrument. *Journal of Teacher Education, 49* (2), 132–139.

National Business Education Association. (1995). *National standards for business education: What America's students should know and be able to do in business.* Reston, VA: National Business Education Association.

Palomba, C. A., & Banta, T. W. (1999). *Assessment essentials.* San Francisco: Jossey-Bass Inc., Publishers.

Tyler, R. (1949). *Basic principles of curriculum and instruction.* Chicago: University of Chicago Press.

U.S. National Commission on Excellence in Education. (1983). *A nation at risk: The imperative for educational reform: A report to the nation and the secretary of education, U.S. Department of Education.* Washington, DC: U.S. Government Printing Office.

Assessment in Content Areas

Wayne A. Moore
Indiana University of Pennsylvania
Indiana, Pennsylvania

The purpose of standards is to specify what a learner should know and be able to do in essential subject areas. Their overall goal is to ensure that students are able to meet the demands and responsibilities of the workplace and to function as knowledgeable citizens and consumers in our global society. While standards are not new to business educators, they have gained increased prominence and urgency in this era of educational accountability.

The *National Standards for Business Education* (NBEA, 1995) has helped provide direction for curriculum development. Business educators can use the standards as a guide to develop content for specific subject areas as well as to formulate assessment tools.

During the past decade, education has seen a transition from traditional assessment to alternative or performance-based assessment techniques. Many business teachers are designing and using innovative assessment strategies. Some of these techniques are called authentic assessment, performance-based assessment, portfolios, exhibits, demonstrations, or profiles. Regardless of the label, each of these techniques has moved beyond the concept of measuring student learning using multiple-choice or other paper-and-pencil tests to a more applied method of evaluation.

The *National Standards for Business Education* can serve as an excellent tool for developing creative assessment materials. This chapter is devoted to providing sample assessments that are based on actual activities used by business teachers who have incorporated the *National Standards for Business*

Education in developing curriculum and in creating assessments related specifically to the standards. Each assessment project ties in at least one achievement standard with one or more performance expectations.

Assessment projects included are from the following areas: accounting, career development, communications, entrepreneurship, information systems, international business, and interrelationships of business functions. Each of the projects can be customized to fit the specific objectives that are being sought. With additional activities, the projects can be the basis for an assessment that covers more than one subject area. The following assessment examples were provided by Pennsylvania business educators.

Accounting

Achievement standard. In the area of accounting process, students will determine the value of assets, liabilities, and owner's equity according to generally accepted accounting principles, explaining when and why they are used.

Performance expectations. Students will define cash, prepare bank reconciliation, establish and maintain petty cash and charge accounts, identify cash control techniques. They will also explain the benefits of electronic fund transfers, automated teller machine transactions, and debit card use.

Overview of activity. The instructor will have a bank officer come to the class with the materials to open a checking account and to discuss the rules and regulations concerning the banking industry. After the guest speaker reviews the banking industry, the students will divide up into groups of three and form a company. They will record banking transactions in a check register and create bank reconciliation. Entries will be made to the cash accounting, and there will be checks to replenish the funds. Students will complete the checks, make deposits with deposit slips using Monopoly money, and record all transactions.

Upon completion of the project, students will be able to explain the operation of petty cash funds and prepare journal entries to record petty cash fund transactions. They will also be able to explain why the bankbook balance of cash should be reconciled and be able to prepare reconciliation.

Materials/equipment. Checkbooks, deposit slips, cash journal, general journal, check register, Monopoly money, deposit slips, ATM cards, and all banking materials. A detailed rubric for this activity is shown in Table 1.

Career Development

Achievement standard. Students will learn about a variety of career opportunities by utilizing career resources. Students will also enhance their oral presentation skills.

Table 1. Rubric for Group Project for the Accounting Process

Criteria	Proficient	Basic	In Progress
Completeness—includes correct petty cash entries	No errors [5 points]	One error [4 points]	Two or more errors [2 points]
Outstanding checks listed	All checks listed [5 points]	One or two checks not listed correctly [4 points]	Three or more checks not listed correctly [2 points]
Deposits recorded	All deposits recorded [5 points]	One deposit not recorded correctly [4 points]	Two or more deposits not recorded correctly [2 points]
Correct formatting of checks	No errors in check format [5 points]	One error in check format [4 points]	Two or more errors in check format [2 points]
Completed reconciliation	Reconciliation with no errors [5 points]	Two or less errors in reconciliation format or totals [4 points]	Three errors in bank reconciliation [2 points]

Total points _____ /25

Overview of activity/performance expectations. Each student is required to research a career he or she would be interested in pursuing. To aid in their choice of a specific career, students may talk to family members and friends about their occupations. It is recommended that each student interview at least two individuals in the career area selected. The student may want to inquire about the following areas of a career:

- Educational background needed;
- What a typical day is like in a particular career;
- Potential for promotions, or career ladder;
- Qualities, characteristics needed to perform job effectively; and
- Advantages/disadvantages of a particular career.

Finally, once the students have gathered information about their chosen careers, each student will be required to prepare a 20-minute oral presentation based on the research collected.

The oral presentation component should include an introduction, body, and conclusion. Students should also be given specific direction to prepare effectively for the presentation. Some student instructions for preparing an oral presentation are listed below:

- Display enthusiasm and interest in the subject; these qualities will maintain the attention and interest of the audience.
- Do plenty of research on the topic. Sufficient knowledge will ensure confidence throughout the presentation. Thorough research will also assist in preparing responses to any audience questions.
- Focus on having good enunciation and pronunciation. Make sure there is continual eye contact and the voice projects to the audience. As always, appropriate grammar needs to be used throughout the presentation.
- Practice the presentation in front of the mirror and friends and/or family. Such practice will build confidence for the day of the presentation.
- Finally, use a visual and/or a one-page handout to enhance the presentation. Refer to the visual during the presentation; provide an explanation so the audience understands the visual/handout. The use of an electronic presentation is recommended. Further instruction about the effective use of an electronic presentation will be discussed in class prior to the due date of this project.
- Review the rubric for a clear understanding of what is expected in this assignment.

Materials/equipment. Computer and presentation screen for PowerPoint presentations, and an overhead projector. Table 2 illustrates a rubric for oral presentation in career research.

Communications

Achievement standard. Students will communicate clear, concise, and correct written directions to their homes.

Performance expectations. Each student will write step-by-step directions using correct spelling, grammar, and mechanics in order to reach his or her home. (Directions start from the school building.) They should

- Write full sentences in a logical, sequential order, using correct punctuation;
- Document landmarks and identifying points along the route;
- Proofread documents to ensure correct grammar, spelling, and punctuation before submitting the final draft;
- Not use slang; and
- After receiving feedback, edit draft to more accurately reflect directions.

Overview of activity. This activity can serve as an excellent entry-level activity for students to enhance their written communication skills. The students

Table 2. Rubric for Oral Presentation for the Career Research Project

Criteria	Exceptional	Met Goal	Did Not Meet Goal
Ability to organize the material	An introduction, body, and conclusion were presented [6 points]	The introduction or conclusion was missing [3 points]	Both the introduction and conclusion were missing [0 points]
Eye contact	Continual eye contact with audience throughout the entire presentation; only referred to notes a few times [6 points]	Needed to refer to notes several times (15 times or more), or had difficulty making direct eye contact with audience; looked at the ceiling or the floor [3 points]	Did not make any eye contact with audience; relied on notes throughout the presentation [0 points]
Use of grammar	No errors [6 points]	One or two errors [3 points]	Had two or more errors [0 points]
Effective use of a visual	Visual was clearly explained, enhancing the presentation [6 points]	Additional explanation regarding visual would have been helpful [3 points]	A visual was not used [0 points]
Ability to respond to questions	Able to respond with logical and well-thought-out answers [6 points]	Knew the answers to the questions, but had difficulty conveying the answers clearly [3 points]	Needed assistance from others to respond to the questions asked [0 points]

Total points _____ /30

must detail the most direct route to their homes. Since they obviously know a great deal about this topic, it provides them the opportunity to focus on the writing aspect. Students are given approximately three days to gather their exact directions and measurements and to determine the fastest route, identify landmarks, etc. On the fourth and fifth days, students write and submit the first official draft. The teacher checks the drafts for errors (spelling, punctuation, and grammar) and returns them the next day for corrections. At the end of the period, the revised drafts are collected.

Over the next week or two, depending on the number of students in the class, the teacher should drive to one or two homes after school each day, using the directions provided by the students. Every detail should be checked for accuracy. The students enjoy this activity, and most are waiting on their porches to see if the teacher will find their houses.

After the teacher has found, or attempted to find, all the houses, the drafts are returned and graded for accuracy and composition. The students edit the drafts according to the instructor's notes and submit a typed final report. The final report then receives the largest portion of the grade.

This activity can cross the curriculum in many ways, allowing for interaction among other teachers and students. It can also be used at different levels in different classes. For example, word processing students can design a brochure with their homes being the main feature. This does not require them to focus as intensely on the directions, but allows them to include other "attractions" close to their homes and to use their creativity to design appealing brochures.

Materials/equipment. Paper, pens, computer if desired.

Entrepreneurship

Achievement standard. Students will identify unique characteristics of an entrepreneur and evaluate the degree to which they possess those characteristics.

Performance expectations. Students will explain and evaluate the primary characteristics of a successful entrepreneur. They will also examine the personal advantages and risks of owning one's own business.

Overview of activity. Toward the beginning of an entrepreneurship course, or a unit on entrepreneurship, have students interview a successful entrepreneur from the community. If the course or unit will eventually have the students completing a business plan, they should interview someone in the same field or industry that their business plan will represent. The interview should be conducted in person if possible.

During the interview, the students are required to ask a set of predetermined questions, as well as questions of their own. Examples of interview questions include

- Why did you start your own business?
- What advice would you give to someone starting his or her own business?
- How did you obtain financing for your business?
- Did you create a business plan? Do you still use it?
- If you have employees, how do you effectively manage them?

- How long have you owned your own business?
- Explain your target market and your marketing strategy.
- What is the legal form of ownership for your business?
- What type of accounting system do you use?
- What impact, if any, has the global marketplace had on your business?
- What sources of assistance does your business use (Small Business Administration, SCORE, etc.)?
- How often do you prepare financial statements?

Upon completion of the interview, the students are to create a PowerPoint presentation. The presentation will then be made to the rest of the class. This project gives students the opportunity to speak with an experienced business owner. They gain a greater appreciation for the process involved in starting up and running a successful business. The students also understand the advantages and risks of starting a business as well as the characteristics of a successful entrepreneur. In addition, the project requires students to work on their presentation skills.

Materials/equipment. Computer with presentation software such as PowerPoint and projection device for computer. A detailed assessment tool is shown in Table 3.

Keyboarding

Achievement standard. Students will use touch-keyboarding skills to enter and manipulate text and data.

Performance expectations. Students will develop touch-keyboarding techniques at acceptable speed and accuracy levels. They will also enter and manipulate numeric data using the touch method on a 10-key pad and identify, compare, and explain features of various keyboards.

Overview of activity. Students will complete a report project with the following components:

- Title Page—The students will include the title, subject, date, name, homeroom number, and advisor's name.
- Report—The students will type a report from copy (no research is needed) utilizing the features of the keyboard including double-spacing, italicizing, boldfacing, centering, widow/orphan control, header function, spell check, tabs, word wrapping, indenting, and proper font.
- Bibliography—The students will type a bibliography from copy to accompany the report using the *Publication Manual of the American Psychological Association* (APA), fourth edition.
- Outline—The students will use the outline feature accompanying the word processing software to produce an outline for the report.

Table 3. Rubric for PowerPoint Presentation

Criteria	Commendable	Acceptable	Unacceptable
Voice quality, diction	Student was easy to understand; correct grammar was used [5 points]	Some words were difficult to understand and/or incorrect grammar was used [3 points]	Could not understand what the speaker was saying; correct grammar not used [0 points]
Poise and appearance	Speaker used gestures effectively, had good eye contact, was self-confident and sure of topic [5 points]	Speaker stood in one spot and rarely looked at the audience; seemed nervous [3 points]	Speaker looked at no one and looked extremely nervous [0 points]
PowerPoint slides	Slides were very well made; effective transitions were utilized; slides were easy to read with lots of white space and no spelling errors [5 points]	No transitions were used; slides were difficult to read with one or more errors [3 points]	Slides were poorly designed and difficult to read with many errors [0 points]
Information	All the necessary questions were addressed; complete information was obtained from the entrepreneur [5 points]	Information presented was incomplete [3 points]	Very little information was presented [0 points]

Total points _____ /20

Materials/equipment. Computers with word processing software, handouts for the report, bibliography, and outline. Table 4 shows a detailed assessment tool.

Information Systems

Achievement standard. Students will identify, select, evaluate, use, install, upgrade, and customize application software. They will also diagnose and solve problems occurring from an application software's installation and use.

Table 4. Rubric for Keyboarding Mastery Report Project

Elements	Outstanding	Satisfactory	Needs Improvement
Title page	Title is centered in caps; information is placed properly; no spelling or grammatical errors [5 points]	One spelling or grammatical error; all information is properly placed on page [3 points]	Two or more spelling or grammatical errors; information not properly placed or missing [1 point]
Report	Typed neatly; no spelling or grammatical errors; boldface, underlining, and italics used; title centered and in caps; double-spaced; header used properly; pages numbered; widow/orphan control used; and font is Courier 12 [5 points]	One to three spelling or grammatical errors; typed neatly; complete and thorough; double-spaced; header and page numbers used properly; widow/orphan control used; and font is Courier 12 [3 points]	Four or more spelling or grammatical errors; not typed neatly; not double-spaced; error in header; page numbers not used; widow/orphan control not on; or wrong font [1 point]
Bibliography	Typed neatly; no spelling or grammatical errors; indent function used; alphabetized by author's last name; double-spaced; followed APA guidelines [5 points]	One or two spelling or grammatical errors; typed neatly; complete and thorough; indent function used; and double-spaced [3 points]	Three or more spelling or grammatical errors; not typed neatly; hanging indent function not used; entries out of order or in wrong style [1 point]
Outline	Outline format used with levels in proper order; title in all caps and centered; main levels typed in all caps; no spelling or grammatical errors [5 points]	Outline format used with levels in proper order; title centered and typed in all caps; one spelling or grammatical error [3 points]	Outline format used improperly; two or more spelling or grammatical errors; title not centered; main levels not typed in all caps [1 point]

Table 4. Rubric for Keyboarding Mastery Report Project (contd.)			
Elements	Outstanding	Satisfactory	Needs Improvement
Miscellaneous	All papers arranged neatly and in proper order; all material handed in within the allotted time frame [5 points]	All papers arranged neatly and in proper order; materials handed in one day late [3 points]	Papers are out of order, not arranged neatly, or two days late; (more than two days late will result in five points deducted for each day late) [1 point]
Comments			
Total points_____ /25			

Activity #1—Analytical thinking and decision making. Students will examine a list of tasks and identify the type of application software needed to complete each task. Then, they will use the catalogs that are provided to identify the specific packages (WordPerfect, Word, Works, etc.) that could be used to complete the tasks. A listing of the system requirements is necessary, but any operating system can be used. Students will examine at least four packages for each task and they will list the operating system requirements, application names, drawbacks, benefits, and justification for the selection of each software package. They will create a form using the computer to compile the information researched. A detailed assessment tool is illustrated in Table 5.

Activity #2—Installing, customizing, and upgrading. Students will install shareware virus protection software on the computer. They will customize the software to scan each disk that enters the system. They will be able to update the software when upgrades become available. Use Table 6 as an assessment tool for this activity.

Activity #3—Creating a newsletter. Students will complete a newsletter project at the end of the unit. They will use the help function, tutorials, and manuals to complete the project. In addition to the basic word processing package images, galleries and templates from other software packages should be used. When software application problems occur while completing the project, students will identify the problems and solve them using the tools available. They should keep a log of the problems and solutions. Table 7 is an example of an assessment tool for this exercise.

Table 5. Software Selection Rubric: Analytical Thinking and Decision Making

Elements	Commendable	Acceptable	Unacceptable
Minimum packages	Identified a minimum of four packages to complete the task [3 points]	Identified only three packages [2 points]	Identified two or less packages [1 point]
Content	Gave drawbacks, benefits, and justification for selecting the packages [5 points]	Justified selection of most of the packages; did not list benefits and drawbacks for all packages [3 points]	Only listed the package selected; did not list justification, drawbacks, or benefits [1 point]
Format	Correct grammar, spelling, and punctuation used [5 points]	Few errors; less than two errors in each area— grammar, spelling, and punctuation [3 points]	Many errors; it is evident proofreading was not done [1 point]
Correct selection	Chose appropriate software packages that would meet the needs to complete each task [5 points]	Choice of packages could be better but they would complete the task; however, others would be better [3 points]	Wrong packages; not appropriate for tasks that were listed [0 points]
Identification	Identified the operating system and requirements to operate the software [2 points]	Identified only operating system or requirements to operate the software [1 point]	Did not identify either requirements or operating system needed [0 points]

Total points_____ /20

International Business

Achievement standard. Students will explain the role of international business and analyze its impact on careers and on doing business at the local, state, national, and international levels.

Performance expectations. Students will demonstrate an awareness of major geographical features of countries around the world. They will identify

Table 6. Software Installation/Customization/Upgrade Rubric

Elements	Acceptable	Unacceptable
Installed software	Installed the software and it functions correctly [5 points]	Installed the software and it is not functional [0 points]
Customized software	Software scans each disk when it enters the system [5 points]	Software is not customized to the specifications listed [0 points]
Updated software	Upgraded the software and it functions properly [5 points]	Upgraded the software and it is not functional [0 points]
Total points_____ /15		

the time zones, major trade regions, and major cities of the world and the countries in which they are located. They will also explain how time zones around the world affect business.

Overview of activity. Students receive instruction in the following areas:

- Seven continents (North America, South America, Europe, Africa, Asia, Australia, and Antarctica);
- Four major ocean divisions (Atlantic, Pacific, Indian, and Arctic oceans);
- Some major trade centers (New York, Chicago, San Francisco, Mexico City, Sydney, London, and others found in various time zones);
- Meridians (lines of longitude); and
- International time zones.

After this instruction, students should label a world map with the above mentioned items according to the detailed assessment tool shown in table 8.

Materials/equipment. The necessary materials (maps, definitions, and locations of cities) are easily found using most electronic sources. Necessary definitions (Greenwich Mean Time [GMT], oceans, meridians, and international time zones) can be found using Microsoft Encarta Encyclopedia or another similar package. The maps are easily found using any electronic atlas (for example, Microsoft Map). An Internet search can be used to find a suitable world map with meridian lines.

Detailed assessment tool. The rubric shown in Table 8 can be revised to include more or less criteria, depending upon the audience. The intended audience is a high school business or entrepreneurship class.

Table 7. Newsletter Rubric

Criteria	Commendable	Acceptable	Unacceptable
Minimum requirements	The newsletter has all the minimum required sections [5 points]	The newsletter is missing only one required section [3 points]	The newsletter is missing more than one section [1 point]
Format	Correct grammar, spelling, and punctuation used [5 points]	Few errors; less than two errors in each area—grammar, spelling, and punctuation [3 points]	Many errors; it is evident proofreading was not done [1 point]
Correct layout	All sections of the newsletter—text and graphics—are spaced evenly; newsletter is balanced and visually appealing [5 points]	The newsletter does not have balance of text and graphics; could have been de-signed in a better manner [3 points]	Layout is done in a random manner; the balance and graphics are poor [1 point]
Problems and solutions	A list of software problems and solutions is included [5 points]	A list is included; however, it is only solutions or problems [3 points]	Did not identify either problems or solutions [1 point]

Total points_____/20

Interrelationships of Business Functions

Achievement standard. Students will describe how cultural differences, export/import opportunities, and current trends in the global marketplace can affect an entrepreneurial venture.

Performance expectations. Students will define culture, develop an understanding of cultural differences, and describe influences of other cultures on American business.

Overview of activity. The assignment is to create a report that appeals to at least three of the senses. The report will communicate cultural facts, unique characteristics, and influences of a particular country. The report must include visual aids that contain text, graphics, pictures, and charts. Also required is a food or ethnic dish popular in that country. This should be available for all students to taste. For the third sense, students will play a sound clip, song, or national anthem originating from the country they researched so that classmates may hear a popular

Table 8. International Business Geography Grading Criteria

Elements	Outstanding	Satisfactory	Unsatisfactory
Continents	Labeled the seven continents with no errors [5 points]	No more than one omission or error [4 points]	Two or more omissions or errors [1 point]
Geographic features	Labeled the four major bodies of water [5 points]	No more than one omission or error [4 points]	Two or more omissions or errors [1 point]
Trade regions	Labeled the major trade centers (from list of cities pro-vided) [5 points]	No more than two omissions or errors [4 points]	Three or more omissions or errors [1 point]
Meridians	Having been given the location of GMT, labeled the latitude lines with no omissions or errors [5 points]	No more than two omissions or errors [4 points]	Three or more omissions or errors [1 point]
Time zones	Having been given the time for GMT, calculated the time and day of the week and date for various cities [5 points]	No more than two omissions or errors [4 points]	Three or more omissions or errors [1 point]
Total points_____/25			

music group or national anthem from each country. The report is worth 70 points. The visual portion of the report will be displayed in the classroom for other students to take notes from and ask questions about.

Materials/equipment. Posterboard, scissors, computers, glue, recipe ingredients, CD player or cassette player. Table 9 shows an assessment tool for this activity.

Summary

The *National Standards for Business Education* provides business educators with an excellent tool for developing course content and assessment materials. Using the standards to create realistic activities that mirror actual

Table 9. Presentation Rubric

Elements	Outstanding	Satisfactory	Unsatisfactory
Content	Information completely accurate; topic well developed, timely; relevant information presented; presentation was engaging and encouraged active learning [10 points]	Some inaccurate information and dated material presented; audience interaction not facilitated [7 points]	Inaccurate information and dated material presented; audience interaction not facilitated [3 points]
Organization	Superb, logical presentation process; easy format to follow and understand [10 points]	Flow of presentation somewhat hard to follow and understand [7 points]	Presentation not logical; format hard to follow [3 points]
Delivery	Correct pronunciation, punctuation, grammar, and tone used; superior voice projection [10 points]	Included one to three errors in pronunciation, spelling, punctuation, or grammar [7 points]	Included four or more errors in pronunciation, spelling, punctuation, or grammar [3 points]
Neatness	Visual aids meticulously prepared; no mistakes, erasures, corrections, smudges, or sloppy handwriting [10 points]	Two or more mistakes, erasures, corrections, or smudges; visual aids haphazardly prepared [7 points]	Three or more mistakes, erasures, corrections, or smudges; hard to read information [3 points]
Business relevance	Presenter effectively illustrated relationships and the effects and relevance of this culture on American business [10 points]	Presenter adequately illustrated relationships and the effects and relevance of this culture on American business [7 points]	Presenter did not illustrate relationships or the effects and relevance of this culture on American business [3 points]

Table 9. Presentation Rubric (contd.)

Elements	Outstanding	Satisfactory	Unsatisfactory
Appendices	Included at least three of the following: charts, tables, graphs, supplementary data [10 points]	Included two or fewer of the following: charts, tables, graphs, supplementary data [7 points]	Included only one of the following: charts, tables, graphs, or other supplementary data [3 points]
Special effects	Many captivating and relevant graphics, pictures, sounds; well-prepared food [10 points]	Minimal or irrelevant graphics, pictures, sounds, and food used [7 points]	No graphics, pictures, sounds, or food used [3 points]
Total points_____ /70			

workplace tasks can help ensure that students have the knowledge and skills necessary for professional success. In order to maximize learning, teachers should give students a variety of real-life activities; these should utilize different learning styles and an array of techniques. The activities should emphasize communication skills, the use of primary sources to stimulate higher-order thinking, and hands-on instruction. In addition, teachers should adjust their instruction according to their experience and input from students. The eight sample assessments presented here are meant to provide ideas for integrating the standards with authentic/performance-based activities. These assessment examples could be used as a template for other learning activities.

References

National Business Education Association. (1995). *National standards for business education: What America's students should know and be able to do in business*. Reston, VA: National Business Education Association.

Assessment in Elementary, Middle, and Junior High School Business Classes

James Russell Smith, Jr.
North Carolina Department of Public Instruction
Raleigh, North Carolina

Business education in elementary, middle, and junior high school has traditionally been concerned with career exploration. The content and courses at these levels permit students to explore various occupations and to become familiar with job preparation requirements, tools, and educational opportunities. In addition, through business education courses, students develop foundational business skills such as keyboarding and computer technology, explore the nature of business in an international economy, and initiate a base for advanced study at the high school level in the fields of business and marketing.

In many states, business education programs or course offerings at the middle level are experiencing tremendous growth. School-to-work legislation has provided for career guidance, exploration, and work-based experiences at all levels. Additionally, the establishment of national career-development guidelines has brought greater general emphasis on workforce development/vocational education from kindergarten through adulthood.

In recent years, a national emphasis on computer/technology skill development for every student has provided business education programs the opportunity to expand beyond the traditional high school classroom to the middle grades/junior high classroom. More and more, keyboarding instruction has moved out of the high school and into the middle/junior level business classes. Courses in computer technology are appearing in the curriculum for middle/junior high school level students in many states, including Mississippi and North Carolina. Administrators have looked to business education teachers to provide and coordinate technology instruction.

While there are growing interests in and opportunities for business education at the elementary and middle/junior high levels, professional literature in this area is almost nonexistent. Likewise, there is a void of research at these levels. Aside from early research on keyboarding skill development, research at the elementary and middle/junior high levels has been neglected by business education. Therefore, this chapter is based primarily on what is commonly known about students at these levels and the initiatives of North Carolina and other states.

Business Education at the Elementary School Level

Historically, the business education curriculum has not included formal "courses" taught at the elementary level. However, the concepts of career development, workplace readiness skills, and basic economic understanding should be integrated throughout the elementary curriculum. In many instances, business educators have provided leadership for the inclusion of these concepts in the elementary school curricula. The integration of business education content can easily take place in the core academic courses of mathematics, science, social studies, and especially the language arts.

Keyboarding, computers, and technology. Keyboarding at the elementary school level is used largely as a vehicle for teaching other subjects, especially the language arts. Research studies in language arts have reported improvements in spelling, composition, reading, knowledge of word meaning, and language usage through keyboarding. Use of the computer at this level motivates interest and improves pupils' attitudes toward their work. The course content of elementary keyboarding reflects the interests and achievement levels of students who compose poems, seasonal greetings, letters to friends, items for school newspapers, descriptions of pets, riddles, answers to questions, and one-word, one-sentence, and multiple-sentence responses to complete a story.

The purpose of teaching elementary students the "touch method" of keyboarding is to provide them with a learning tool to use in other classes. Without appropriate keyboarding instruction, students will develop, or have already, their own methods of keyboarding. Prigge (1993) suggests that students enrolling in "courses after using computers in the elementary grades without proper instruction have a difficult time unlearning their bad habits of hunting and pecking, which causes student frustration." Warner, Behymer, and McCrary (1992) observe, "hunting and pecking requires conscious attention to what the fingers are doing. Consequently, students spend more time concentrating on how to keyboard than on the material they are composing. Students who are capable of touch keyboarding can concentrate on problem solving and composing rather than on mechanics."

In grades K–2, Jackson and Berg (1986) suggest appropriate objectives include keyboard familiarity with emphasis placed on locating keys, using correct fingers, and learning the position of home row keys. By the third grade, the objectives focus on the development and application of correct keyboarding techniques. As students progress, objectives expand to include correct keying techniques for the number, symbol, and function keys. At this age, software applications are largely point and click. However, in the upper elementary grades, students should be introduced to simple word processing and other application packages, such as basic spreadsheets, databases, presentation graphics, desktop publishing, and telecommunications.

Assessment for keyboarding instruction at the elementary level is primarily formative instead of summative. The modeling and evaluation of correct technique should be the responsibility of all teachers using the keyboard as a tool for learning. The use of a simple technique check sheet ensures students will exhibit correct posture, keystroking, spacing, and use of the shift key, as well as fluid motions. Good technique is a prerequisite to sound skill development.

Elementary school students can learn touch keyboarding and can use the computer as a communication tool. However, formal keyboarding instruction is offered at the elementary level on a very limited basis partly because of the lack of business teachers trained to teach keyboarding at this level and the unavailability of funds to purchase equipment and pay teachers.

Career exploration and workplace skills. At the elementary level, exploration of careers means helping students become aware of the world of work, the values of a work-oriented society, and the role of the individual. Business educators serve as a resource person for classroom teachers, providing information about careers in the broad realm of business and marketing. Career concepts should be integrated into the daily activities of students so they may become aware of how skills learned in traditional settings, such as communication and computational skills, are applied in business and marketing careers. Examples of how academic skills can be reinforced through occupational settings include the following:

- Teaching students the value of money by giving them control over a set amount of funds. Children should be allowed to budget and make purchases with a preset limit on spending.
- Helping students develop a strong awareness of self. Students should be encouraged to talk about their feelings in terms of goals, values, wishes, interests, likes and dislikes, and personal strengths. Students may illustrate these feelings in the form of a scrapbook or journal.
- Diversifying the classroom by assigning responsibilities based on achievement rather than gender. Teachers should help students become aware of biases—gender, ethnic, racial, etc. They should treat every student as a special and unique individual.
- Helping students cultivate basic competencies such as speaking skills, writing ability, and basic math skills through homework, independent classroom work, and group activities.

Assessment of workplace skills need not be separate from the assessment of academic skills being taught at the elementary level. When students begin to see the connections between school and the world of work, their achievement level rises, thus making the elementary experience more meaningful (Christ, 1995).

Business Education at the Middle/Junior High School Level

One of the goals of education at all levels is preparation for work regardless of the individual's career objective. At the middle/junior high school level, the career education emphasis is on exploration, which involves examining career pathways in relation to one's interests, abilities, aptitudes, and values. Using available goals and objectives as guides, the teacher develops specific objectives for the local school, making adaptations as needed on the basis of the school's unique characteristics and needs.

The physical, social, psychological, and intellectual characteristics of middle grade students differ from those of secondary students. They are often moody and loud, displaying markedly different reactions and behavior patterns to the same stimuli. Realism and facts fascinate students at this age. They begin to question the right of adults to dominate and they seek prestige. Most enjoy group enterprises, but find some satisfaction in working alone. Socially, youth are acquiring adult roles through trial and error (Atwell, 1998).

The business education classroom can provide excellent opportunities for students to explore and assume, temporarily or through simulated activities, their adult roles. Psychologically, this is the period during which youth acquire an identity. They narrow and focus their personal, occupational, sexual, and ideological commitments to the point where they are perceived by others to be adults. Intellectually, they come to school knowing more than previous generations and possessing greater intellectual sophistication.

Middle grade/junior high students exhibit a wide range of interests. This is the time when the mind is developing to its adult capacity. Business education teachers need to be aware of these characteristics and to use them as a guide in developing a career-exploration program involving the business and marketing occupations. The organization of topics should reflect opportunities in the state, regional, and national employment communities. Areas of emphasis include an examination of the career field, skills and knowledge needed, the occupational outlook and career ladders, real and simulated work based experiences, self-assessment, and decision making. A variety of group and individual activities are appropriate for meeting individual needs.

Keyboarding, computers, and technology. Research indicates that middle/junior high school students have the developmental skills needed for keyboard learning, making it easier for them to acquire the skill. At this age,

Erickson (1993) states, "they [students] are risk takers; that is, they are ready to make the effort needed to force their speed to the highest possible levels." Keyboarding and technology skill development offered as separate courses at the middle/junior high school level primarily focus on personal and academic use—keying letters, reports, charts, graphs; organizing data, e-mail; and developing Internet search skills. Other objectives include learning proper use and care of equipment, enhancing keyboard fluency, keying assignments in other courses, developing composition skills, and improving proofreading ability.

Assessment at the middle/junior high level is a combination of formative and summative evaluations. The classroom teacher uses both types of evaluations to diagnose weaknesses, to measure achievement in terms of course objectives, to motivate students, and to serve as a basis of determining grades. Again, as at the elementary level, good technique should be stressed, observed, and evaluated using a technique check sheet. Students should be given a copy of the rating scale or one should be displayed in the keyboarding classroom so they know the techniques and work habits on which they are being evaluated.

Also, as in any learning situation, it is important for learners to be able to assess their progress. Business and industry wants individuals to be able to assess their performance and make adjustments to meet established goals and objectives. In order to do this, it is vital that clear outcomes be established, modeled, and communicated. Students must be able to "picture" successful performance in their minds. As good techniques become established habits, the evaluation may be stressed to a lesser degree.

Summative evaluations include knowledge and performance tests. Knowledge tests measure whether a student knows basic information such as formatting rules, proofreading symbols, equipment parts, parts of various documents, and applications performed by different software. Performance tests are used to measure students' keystroking ability and the application of basic skills to problem-solving situations. Timed writings and production tests are examples of performance tests.

Regardless of the method of measurement and evaluation, criteria must specify precisely the expected student performance and behavior in the form of objectives. It is essential that students know these expectations from the beginning of the course in order for them to focus on current learning outcomes and transfer these outcomes to future learning.

Career exploration and workplace skills. Learning to conduct a career search and to identify career interests should be an important part of every student's middle level experience. Today's changing business world and economic environment dictate the necessity of beginning career exploration at an early age. The objectives of career exploration at the middle/junior high school level are achieved through separate courses taught by business educators as well as content integrated into core or academic courses. In a well-planned middle level experience, each teacher, whether academic or vocational, should assume responsibility for establishing career development concepts.

The *National Standards for Business Education* (NBEA, 1995) suggests several areas of emphasis that can be incorporated into the career exploration curriculum:

- Assessment of personal strengths and weaknesses as they relate to career exploration and development.
- Utilization of career resources to develop an information base that includes global occupational opportunities.
- Relation of work ethic, workplace relationships, workplace diversity, and workplace communication skills to career development.
- Application of knowledge gained from individual assessment to a comprehensive set of goals and an individual career path.
- Development of strategies to make an effective transition from school to work.
- Relation of the importance of lifelong learning to career success.

Assessment in middle/junior high school tends to be more structured than at the elementary level. Assessment at this level focuses on two major areas—student and program-level achievement. Student evaluation focuses on content, activities, interests, values, attitudes, and processes. Content tests emphasize knowledge of an occupational cluster. Activities, including role-playing, simulations, hands-on experiences, and work-based learning experiences, are important tools through which students learn about the world of work.

Observation of student activities can also offer the classroom teacher a means of assessing student performance. However, too much emphasis must not be placed on grading these activities. The intent is for students to explore, not to master specific skills and knowledge. Again, teachers must clearly establish and communicate learning outcomes to their students.

For many middle grades/junior high students, assessments of interests and processes are new experiences. Interests, values, and attitudes checklists and rating scales may be used both as pre- and postassessments to reflect student change. These should not be used for grading purposes, but as a means of having students examine change in their personal behaviors and attitudes.

Decision-making skills are best measured through application problems in which students are expected to arrive at decisions using the techniques learned in class. Evaluation of this or other decisions is based on students' abilities to follow a logical decision-making process and to arrive at a reasonable conclusion. The process is more important than a correct answer.

Work habits, attitudes, and interpersonal relationships are vital to overall job performance. The classroom teacher may want to establish businesslike criteria for classroom performance, such as promptness, neatness, the ability to follow directions and work without disturbing others, and so on, as a means for evaluating student behavior in the course. Both the students and the teacher should complete checklists.

Program assessment at the middle/junior high level should incorporate several types of evaluation as an ongoing component of the career exploration program. The changing nature of business and marketing careers, both in emerging occupations and existing jobs, necessitates frequent examination of the content of the exploration program to assure an accurate representation of the job market in the business and marketing fields.

Advisory committees composed of representatives from business and industry, as well as parents and community representatives, can help the business education teacher in program assessment. The business education teacher is responsible for keeping up-to-date on employment opportunities and the nature of business-related jobs. Publications from national, state, and local labor departments are helpful in assessing the current job market.

Summary

"Career development differs from traditional curriculum in that it encompasses an individual's total lifestyle—education, occupation, social responsibility, and leisure" (NBEA, 1995). As technology continues to change the nature of work and new organizational patterns alter the workplace, career decision making assumes an elevated priority in the student's educational experience. Career development instruction should be integrated throughout the student's educational experiences, especially at the elementary and middle levels.

Students should begin learning about the world of work by examining workplace requirements and job expectations in the elementary grades. This early exposure is done best by integrating the content into the core academic curricula. As students progress to the middle/junior high levels, instruction and skill development become more specific to particular jobs in the business and marketing fields. A system of career development education should be formulated and integrated into the entire curriculum at all academic levels and continued as a lifelong process. This system includes traditional as well as nontraditional methodology such as mentoring, shadowing, community service, cooperative education, and school-to-work transition. Business educators should play a major role in the development and implementation of this system.

Keyboarding has become a life skill that allows people to be proficient in using technology as a tool for personal and professional reasons. With the increased use of the computer and other technology in every aspect of our daily lives, it is essential that all students, regardless of their career aspirations, receive instruction to become proficient and effective users of technology. For now, keyboarding is a critical skill for all students to possess.

The need for research in business education at the elementary and middle/junior high levels is apparent. Now that introductory computer/technology instruction is becoming the norm rather than exception at the middle/junior high school level, more research needs to be conducted to ensure that age-appropriate strategies and techniques are being used to effectively teach and assess these skills. Broader areas of research in business education may address the following questions:

- How should business education be articulated throughout a student's educational experience—from kindergarten through adulthood?
- What contribution can business education make in relation to the National Career Development Guidelines?
- How are keyboarding and technology skills best developed at the elementary and middle school levels? Who should provide this instruction?
- What role can/should business education play in school-to-work transition?

Business education instruction at the elementary, middle, and junior high levels is quickly becoming the source from which students acquire keyboarding and computer/technology skills and an introduction to careers. Today, more than ever, articulation at every level of education is important. Business educators at all levels should envision a comprehensive progression of skills from kindergarten to 12th grade and beyond. By embracing rather than resisting this change, business educators are destined to remain strong and vital participants in the education of all students.

References

Atkinson, J., & Kimbrell, G. (1998). *Exploring business and computer careers* (2nd ed.). Cincinnati, OH: West Educational Publishing.

Atwell, N. (1998). *In the middle—New understandings about writing, reading, and learning* (2nd ed.). Portsmouth, NH: Boynton/Cook Publishers.

Brown, B. L. (1999). School-to-work and elementary education. *Practice Application Brief* (No. 5). Washington, DC: ERIC Clearinghouse on Adult, Career, and Vocational Education, Center on Education and Training for Employment, The Ohio State University.

Christ, G. M. (1995). Curriculums with real-world connections. *Educational Leadership, 52* (8), 32–35.

Erickson, L. (1993). *Basic keyboarding guide for teachers.* Cincinnati, OH: South-Western Publishing Company.

Jackson, T., & Berg, D. (1986). Elementary keyboarding—Is it important? *The Computing Teacher, 13* (6), 8.

National Business Education Association. (1995). *National standards for business education: What America's students should know and be able to do in business.* Reston, VA: National Business Education Association.

National School-to-Work Learning and Information Center. (1996). Career development in school-to-work. *Resource Bulletin.* Washington, DC: National School-to-Work Learning and Information Center.

National School-to-Work Learning and Information Center. (1997). School-to-work in elementary schools. *Resource Bulletin.* Washington, DC: National School-to-Work Learning and Information Center.

North Carolina Department of Public Instruction. (1997). *Business Computer Technology.* Raleigh, NC: Workforce Development Education.

North Carolina Department of Public Instruction. (1998). *Keyboarding: Middle grades.* Raleigh, NC: Workforce Development Education.

North Carolina Department of Public Instruction. (1999). *Classroom assessment: Linking instruction and assessment.* Raleigh, NC: Instructional Services.

North Carolina Department of Public Instruction. (1999). *Exploring business technologies: Business and marketing.* Raleigh, NC: Workforce Development Education.

Prigge, L. (1993). Beyond Keyboarding for Elementary Students. *Mountain-Plains Business Education Association (Service Bulletin No. 36),* 20.

Warner, K., Behymer, J., & McCrary, S. (1992, October). Two points of view on elementary school keyboarding. *Business Education Forum, 47* (1), 27–28.